Restless

in

Peace

About the Author

Mariah de la Croix (Phoenix, AZ) has interacted with spirits since she was less than one year old. A licensed cremationist and embalmer, she spent over five years working in various funeral homes. Currently, she teaches others how to sense and interact with spirits.

A Psychic Mortician's Encounters
with Those Who Refuse to Rest

Restless

in

Peace

Mariah de la Croix

Llewellyn Publications
Woodbury, Minnesota

FIRST EDITION
First Printing, 2012

Cover art © Woman: iStockphoto.com/Maria Pavlova
        Turquoise background: iStockphoto.com/enviromantic
        Halloween cobweb: iStockphoto.com/Susan Trigg
        Coffin: Ocean Photography/Veer
Cover design by Ellen Lawson
Editing by Rosemary Wallner
"Sharp Dressed Man" used by kind permission of Stage Three Music (BMI). All
    rights administered by BMG Rights Management (US) LLC.

Llewellyn Publications is a registered trademark of Llewellyn Worldwide Ltd.

Library of Congress Cataloging-in-Publication Data
De la Croix, Mariah, 1958–
  Restless in peace : a psychic mortician's encounters with those who refuse to rest /
Mariah de la Croix. — 1st ed.
      p. cm.
  ISBN 978-0-7387-3068-4
1. De la Croix, Mariah, 1958– 2. Spiritualism—Biography. I. Title.
  BF1283.D4425A3 2012
  133.9'1—dc23
                        2012016659

Llewellyn Publications
A Division of Llewellyn Worldwide Ltd.
2143 Wooddale Drive
Woodbury, MN 55125-2
www.llewellyn.com

Printed in the United States

DEDICATION

I hereby dedicate this book to all of my animals:
past, present, and future.
Without their love, compassion, vision, and strength
I would have never been able to see beyond
the veil.
May your lives be long and happy. May your spirits rise.
Love never dies.

Contents

Acknowledgments

Without the help of many kind and hard-working people, this book would never have come to pass. It is here that I would like to thank them for all their hard work, inspiration, suggestions, guidance, and support.

I would like to thank my editors—Amy Glaser, acquisitions editor at Llewellyn Worldwide, and Rosemary Wallner—whose insights and vision of my rough drafts kept this book from being nothing more than a dream. Also, a person who started out as a client and has become a dear friend, D.C., has helped in so many little ways with some of the wording in this book, bringing simple solutions to problems that didn't need to become bigger than they were. Thank you, dear ladies.

Kyt Dotson and Johnna Gale, two beautiful and talented souls, writers, and friends, gave me inspiration to write and showed me that putting thoughts and words onto paper can be appreciated by other people besides me.

Thanks go out to my dearest friend and buddy, John E., who has stuck by my side through thick and thin, helping my life in ways he can't imagine. He has been there for me with his comments and insights on my retelling of spirit encounters that showed me this book is more than just a sharing of experiences, it is also an affirmation that our lives here aren't wasted.

Many heartfelt thanks go to my dear and wonderful neighbors, P, C, and M, for their help on chapter title work and their kind ear in listening to my frustrations when I was at a loss for words. The value of their encouragement, again, puts me at a loss for words except for one—priceless!

To my mother, Hazel, and my daughter, M.C., I thank you both for showing me visions of life that were both youthful and trying at times—your strength has been one of your greatest gifts to me.

And, finally, to my husband I give loving thanks and warmth for his stubbornness, his all-too-often quiet responses that told me more than I wanted to know, and his pushy attitude that made me sit and get this book done. Without you, dear man, and without the energies of all mentioned here, this book would never have come to be. Without you all, and without the vision of Llewellyn Worldwide, my adventures with spirits would have stayed locked in my memories. To you I humbly bow and give great thanks.

I cannot forget and wish to also thank those who have gone before us. Even though their names along with the names of locations and other people involved have all been changed to protect them—alive and dead—they, our ancestors, are the real reason this book exists. To all the spirits in this book, I give my greatest and most heartfelt thanks. Bless you. May you all rest in peace.

THE OPENING
OF THE CASKET

Welcome to my parlor. I am Mariah de la Croix and I'm a mortician. I saw the dead in their true, corpse-like state on a daily basis. For nearly five years, I worked in this highly respectable profession until severe illness took my abilities away, suddenly, and with little warning. I saw and worked with the bodies of the dead, and I also interacted with their spirits that chose to remain in the various funeral homes, crematories, and cemeteries I worked in or visited. I found their reasons for remaining to be as different and as unique as they were in life.

I hadn't prepared myself for the possibility of these encounters in my work life, but I should have known better, as I have communicated with spirits all of my life in many different ways. My earliest recollection of interaction was at the age of just eighteen months. I vividly recall being secured in my light green, steel tube-legged high-chair and playing with a little toy when I became aware of the aroma of butter melting in the oatmeal my dad was preparing for my breakfast. Due to my youth, I couldn't express to him that butter made me feel nauseated and that I wanted him to keep it out of my food. I tried to no avail to get his attention and ask him, in some way, not to include the butter. My frustration grew, along with the nausea in my tummy, when the unseen hands of a couple who resided with us in spirit picked up my chair with me in it, and lovingly placed it immediately behind my father working diligently at the stove. I was then able to get his attention by tugging on his shirt, which caused him to jump into the air and turn around ready to pounce.

His laughter filled the air after his initial shock wore off. He kept the butter out of my oatmeal and had no qualms about my movement across the room. Dad knew the spirit couple had moved me because he too interacted with spirits living in that house—as did my mother and sister.

I was fortunate in being raised in a household where spirits and the paranormal were normal topics of conversation at the dinner table. Spirits and entities of many types and personalities often manifested in various ways in the houses we lived in. I became familiar with them—friendly with some, wary with others—as they were just a part of our lives like any other roommate. These frequent visits from the other side gave me a healthy appreciation for those who have died, along with a spiritually empathic connection that has sometimes warned me about an upcoming danger, but has occasionally gotten me into trouble too.

When I was a teenager, my family and I moved from the northern Midwest to the southwestern desert region of the United States. I found the new energies and spirits of the desert to be foreign to me, with wonderfully different feelings than what I had been used to. While in high school, a spirit alerted me that something odd was going to happen to my sister. My attention had been drawn to windows but upon investigation I found nothing. I heard sounds of scraping or breathing near windows. When I walked toward them, I often entered a chilled cloud of air containing the scent of my sister's perfume. Spirits had never communicated with me in such cryptic messages before. My mother and sister were as confused as I was about their messages and their references to windows.

However, several months later we found out a peeping Tom was stalking my sister and looking at her through her bedroom window. That was the message the spirit was trying to send, and I felt horrible that I couldn't decipher its meaning sooner to spare my sister the fright and embarrassment she experienced.

During those high school years, I experienced the deaths of several family members and friends. I became attracted to the surroundings of the funeral establishments and the various energies in them, while also being drawn to the feelings of the survivors in their bereavement and grief— whether cold and standoffish or emotional and involved.

The dead were no problem, be they relative or friend. I often felt their presence and could give messages to those who were hurting. Sometimes those messages were appreciated and sometimes they were disdained; but I gave them anyway, with love and compassion that has stayed with me to this very day.

After high school, I decided to live somewhat of a normal life and put my ability to communicate with spirits to rest. That didn't work. Throughout a bad marriage of two years, my then-husband and I both had encounters with spirits—most of which would show him what they thought of his abuse toward me by tossing him down the stairs or dismantling his radio-controlled airplanes that he spent a great deal of time and energy building. He also interacted with and saw spirits, sometimes more often than I, but he would not heed their advice or warnings. Our divorce in the late 1970s was a welcome respite from many things.

Years later, I was privileged to give birth to a beautiful daughter who is also able to communicate with spirits. She often did so when she was little and accompanied me to various homes. I ran a business where I saw to the needs of people who required specialized care and cleaning help, often with a great deal of discretion. At these locations, I was glad to have the company of the various spirits that inhabited them. When my daughter came to work with me, she would tell me about the children and other spirits that resided there, often playing with them for hours as I saw to the chores of the house and grounds.

Sometimes the spirits in these houses were just going through the motions of what they had done in life. I learned to expect these residual hauntings at regular times. One woman's spirit returned every year, just before Christmas, with her arms loaded with packages, placing them in a front closet that was long gone. Some residual hauntings were connected with high-stress events, such as the sound of a gun being fired accompanied by the scent of gunpowder. In one house this occurred on the yearly anniversary of the death of someone whose life had been taken due to an unfortunate altercation.

Some homes had full hauntings connected with severe weather or an upcoming death, such as the spirit of a woman who would be seen, heard, and smelled only when the phone was going to ring—letting the family know that someone close to them had died. This spirit was more of a harbinger of death, but when we became aware of her presence, the family and I always knew that the phone would ring—we just didn't know for whom.

While running my own business and taking care of private homes, my body began to slowly tell me something was going wrong. Doctors performed myriads of tests, came up with nothing, and told me I was getting older. I realized I would soon have to forego the physical work I loved, so I had better get back to school and find another profession before it was too late. I wanted to utilize all the talents I'd developed over the years working for many types of individuals in some very unique ways. I entered college and began taking my core classes of English and math while

I researched which field would be best suited for me. After long and hard study, I decided to enter the mortuary field.

I obtained a two-year degree, which is suitable for the southwestern state in which I reside. I had to finish all my prerequisite classes in two years instead of one because I worked two jobs, one still helping people in their homes and the other as a funeral attendant in a local mortuary. My last year of college was tough, with little time to rest as I attended class full time, drove four hours round trip from home to school, then to my first job taking care of houses, then on to the mortuary where my evenings didn't end until nearly midnight many nights. This went on for a full year. Little did I know that the physical stress was awakening in me something that had lain dormant in my DNA.

The stress began to lift after graduation. I had my diploma and degree in hand, passed the National Funeral Board exams with flying colors, was certified as an embalmer so that I could now intern, and also became a licensed cremationist. I began working full time in a second funeral home as an apprentice director and licensed intern embalmer. During that year's internship, I met with families, supervised viewings, embalmed, did a few cremations, did some more embalming, removed bodies from various locations (many of which I embalmed), and often was on call answering the phone at all hours of the night.

After obtaining my full license as an embalmer, I had just one more year to go before becoming a fully licensed funeral director. Unfortunately, the stress on my body, the exposure to chemicals, and the heavy lifting of full caskets and bodies took its toll on my health. Every embalming was a work of art to me, but every embalming made it harder and harder for my body to recuperate. I was in constant pain and it showed. Doctors still performed tests and said that I had just gotten too old or needed a vacation. Family and friends tried to help, but soon began to go along with the doctors in telling me it was all in my head.

The spirits at the funeral homes in which I worked or filled in knew differently, though. They made me laugh and comforted me when I was blue because my body was not working right. The spirits kindly told me to leave before my body gave out or I would be forced onto their side before my time. On a June afternoon in 2009, just a few months before I would have obtained my full license as a funeral director, a spirit approached me after I'd received the body of someone I had known in life. Spirit asked me why I was still there and why I kept pushing myself so hard. He informed me, in no uncertain terms, that I too would be on that shelf in the cooler if I kept this up. I had a hard decision to make. Within two weeks' time, I walked away from a profession that I dearly loved.

Many family members whom I have helped over the five years I was active contacted me after I left, suggesting I write about my experiences. Some of these people are also sensitive with spirits and are mediums themselves. They knew I had much to share that would entrance and entertain. Spirits I had encountered in the funeral homes and cemeteries came into my home and encouraged me in their own ways. They entered my dreams, made pads of paper and pens fall on the floor, and opened the word processing software on my computer. One even called me on the phone and said one word—write! Others helped me to open my sensitivities and learn to help others, while also helping myself. When I graduated from college, I took the funeral directors' oath—I took an oath to the dead and to the living. I haven't turned my back on that and I never will.

Out of consideration for the great necessity for privacy and respect for the living and the dead, I have changed all the names of the spirits and my co-workers as well as the various funeral homes, crematories, and cemeteries. With humility and grace, honor and dignity, I now share with you my encounters with those who aren't quite ready to rest in peace.

So, would you be so kind as to now follow me into the parlor where many await...

CHAPTER 1

THE DOORMAN

Sometimes we are blessed to meet people who enjoy doing their jobs and are highly dedicated to them along with the people they serve, no matter how tedious or mundane their jobs may seem to others. There are also those individuals who, after death, keep that dedication alive. Unfortunately, when we run into this dedication we don't always see it as a blessing. If a spirit is nearby, we often become nervous or apprehensive, no matter where the spirit is located or what it's doing. When the location of the manifestation is a mortuary, we may try to figure out why they are there once we've taken the time to calm down.

Such was the case with an encounter I had in one particular room of the first funeral home I worked at. Serenity Shores Mortuary was the largest and busiest facility in the area. The main building held a labyrinth of offices, arrangement rooms, hallways, chapels, parlors, and preparation areas for the bodies. A long, back hall corridor used only by employees was also in the building. If you walked in either direction through the white, almost blinding walls, you would pass many doors that led to offices, small storage closets, a prep room, flower room, dressing room, and kitchen.

About halfway down this exceptionally long hallway, there was a room with a smaller room inside of it. The larger room, for the most part, was storage for office supplies, cleaning materials, light bulbs for the chapels, flower stands, and casket liners along with the rental caskets used for viewing the dead prior to a cremation. There was also room to store one very important item: the bodies of the deceased patiently waiting preparation for viewing or cremation. They were held in the cooler, the little room inside of the larger room. The cooler was a walk-in, galvanized metal room. The door to the cooler was the same as any used on a large, walk-in refrigerator; it was very thick, well-insulated, and always securely latched to keep in the cold. Due to the presence of the cooler in the storage room, we nicknamed the entire space *the cooler room*.

The cooler room had a large and heavy fire door that connected it to the long hallway. The door was massive at seven feet high, four to five inches thick, and well over three feet wide. It weighed at least sixty pounds and was supported on four massive steel hinges mounted in an equally strong and formidable steel doorframe bolted into thick, brick walls. The door opened inward into the cooler room and was out of the way of the employee hallway. During the day, as we rushed in and out of the room with our arms loaded with supplies or moving caskets, we kept the massive door open. Breezes from air conditioning vents and heater ducts didn't hit this door, and it wasn't easily jarred when left open due to its weight, so we all felt safe and comfortable in leaving that cooler room door open.

Whenever I walked into the storage room area of the cooler room to get a trash bag or light bulb or check the temperature of the cooler itself, I soon learned to pay attention to that door.

I had only worked at Serenity Shores for a few weeks when that door moved by itself for the first time. I had gone into the room to get some trash bags for cleanup after a late-night visitation, also known as a viewing. My back was to the door when I heard shuffling footsteps behind me. I thought my friend and co-worker, Agnes, was there. While working on getting the bags out of the box, I called out, "Hey! Do you need some bags or was your family nice and neat for you?" There was no reply. Then the lights in the room flickered. They never went off, they just flickered. I stood up all the way, with my back still to the door, and gazed at the overhead lights as I froze with a feeling of panic as a shiver moved up my spine. My throat tightened up with fear and I stayed still for the few seconds that the lights flickered. I made myself shake off the panicked feeling and thought, "Fine. I just start working in a funeral home with a bunch of dead people and I start freaking out over nothing. Gotta be just a loose bulb." I shook my head while quietly giggling at myself.

I turned around and didn't see Agnes. I was still thinking that we had a short in the ceiling light or the air-conditioning had kicked in, causing a power drain. A person has to come up with logical explanations for things like this, and I always try. But this time I was stumped, especially when I remembered the sound of the shuffling feet. As all the lights were now on and stable, I walked over to the cooler and, upon opening its door, found it empty. After securing the cooler's door I proceeded into the hall and saw no one there either or in the kitchen. I opened the door and found it empty. I moved to the main doorway and looked up and down the hall and into the kitchen; I saw no one.

I took my trash bags into the lobby of the other chapel where I heard people speaking and knew a family was still visiting their loved one. I looked for Agnes and saw her sitting comfortably in an overstuffed chair at the far end of the lobby, patiently reading a book about her newest hobby—origami. Even though this woman was less than five feet tall and more than ninety years young, she got around better and worked harder than someone in their forties. I quietly signaled for her to come over to where I stood.

"Were you just in the cooler room?" I whispered.

"Nope," she replied as her big, blue eyes gazed up at me through her reading glasses. She looked down at the bags in my hand and whispered, "That's nice of you to bring me some bags. I'm going to need them. They've gone through eight boxes of tissues in just the past two hours. Thanks." As she took the bags out of my hand, I told her what had just happened in the cooler room. She shook her hand near her ear while turning her head from side to side and whispered not to worry about that; it happened all the time. I thought that was good to know, but wondered what she meant.

I was so preoccupied due to what she had said that I did not realize she had taken all the bags. I was halfway into my own empty chapel before realizing I did not have in my hand what I had left the chapel to get. I stopped dead in my tracks when it dawned on me that I would have to go back into the cooler room, alone, to get more bags. Feeling like a child, I stomped my foot and whined, "I don't wanna!"

When I reached the cooler room, the lights were now off. I stood scratching my head, knowing they'd been left on. Flicking on the light switch and walking in to get my bags for the second time, I again heard the shuffling footsteps behind me near the door. Turning slowly to look toward the sound, I saw nothing other than the large fire door. Suddenly, the lights dimmed to near darkness. I quickly turned back to the box of bags and frantically grabbed a handful. I then heard the sound of a man clearing his throat just as I was turning around and making my way toward the door. The sound wasn't far away. The door I approached began to slowly close. My feet quickly moved. I wanted to be away from that room and didn't want to be alone.

When I got into the hall, I turned around, backing out in the direction of the kitchen and my chapel. Wanting to keep a close eye on the cooler room, I didn't pay attention to what or who may have been behind me and backed into

Agnes. I squealed like a little girl and jumped a foot in the air when I bumped into her. After catching my breath and laughing at myself, she stated that she had just come in to get more tissues for her family, saw me backing down the hallway, and wondered why. I let her know what had happened in the cooler room.

"Yes, I know. Watch it in there," she said as she set her jaw and took a quick glance toward the room. "Now, I'm not going to talk about it no more so don't ask me nothin'." She was emphatic, so my only choice was to get back into my chapel and finish my job for the night.

More than an hour later, while we were both walking out to our cars, she let me know that she did not want to talk about the cooler room in any way, shape, or form. I was not to bring it up to anyone either. Since I was new, not only to the profession but also to Serenity Shores, I decided to keep quiet, listen, and learn.

Several days later, I was fortunate to work again, this time with a full crew on duty. The hustle and bustle of the mortuary was nonstop. Families and services were everywhere. Flowers lined the back halls, waiting their turn to stand vigil around the caskets of those who had passed on. Urns full of cremains were lined up like corpulent soldiers waiting to go off sentry duty. The other employees and I buzzed about, setting up the chapels and parlors for services, proofreading the memorial print material, typing death certificates, preparing bodies for the crematory, and making a lot of coffee.

I watched as my fellow employees went in and out of the cooler room with no incidents. I began to think that the previous incident must have been a fluke or a touch of whimsy. I went into the cooler room for tissues and trash bags for the evening's visitations; nothing happened in the room other than the door slowly closing after I'd fully entered it. I explained that away as a draft caused by my walking into the room; the little bit of chill I felt in the air must have been from the cooler. I kept my eye on the door as I found my supplies and left before the door had a chance to fully close. As I passed the kitchen, I saw several directors taking a break and enjoying some coffee. I thought about asking them if they had had any problems with the cooler room door closing on its own. I decided against it, remembering Agnes' advice a few nights earlier. I went on about my business setting up the many floral arrangements that had arrived for the night's visitations.

That evening went smoothly, with both families pleased and comforted by our service and attention. The family Agnes attended to had decided to cut their evening short and vacated the building before mine did. Agnes was tired, but volunteered to stay to help clean up. I let her know that I would be fine alone and she could be comfortable in going home. Before she left, she checked everywhere except where I needed to work and secured the remainder of the building. All I had to do was straighten up my chapel, set up things for the morning, lock up for the night, dump the trash, and go home. Not bad. Now, where had I placed those trash bags?

I knew I had grabbed some earlier and distinctly remembered placing them on the piano bench in my chapel's music room. Wanting to avoid the cooler room when the building was nearly empty, I had made sure to put a stack of bags in my chapel. Now they were nowhere to be found. Leaving my family alone and leaving that chapel was not an option at that time, as my family was beginning to say their final good-byes to their loved one and I needed to be there to assist, if necessary, and to show them out. I had to suck it up, act like a grownup, and get my trash bags. So after everyone left, and the only two folks left in the chapel were the person in the casket and myself, I did just that.

I locked the doors of the chapel and slowly proceeded up the aisle toward the casket to make a right turn toward the interior hallway that led to the cooler room with the crazy door. While walking up that aisle, I talked to myself confidently and assured myself that everything would be fine; whatever had happened the other night was nothing. I gathered my courage to lay claim to my trash bags. Nothing would frighten me now.

I was fine walking down the interior hallway past the kitchen, but upon entering the cooler room I immediately became aware of the deathly quiet that now dominated. Earlier, the room had been buzzing from the noise and organized chaos of the entire building bleeding through the room's brick walls, but now the silence engulfed me like a cloak. I found this a little eerie, but pressed on. I went to the shelves to get my bags and heard the feet shuffling behind me again. Looking over my shoulder, I saw the cooler room door begin to close. With bags in hand, I made a fast dash for the door and decided to shut it myself and be done with this nonsense. When I put my hand on the knob, it felt colder than ice. I tried pulling the door shut but it would not move. It was as if someone was holding it. I pulled the door a few inches away from the wall and immediately felt it being pulled back toward the wall. This tug-of-war was played three times before I realized what was going on. I let go of the knob, made a fast retreat from the cooler room, and went back into my chapel. With my heart racing, hands shaking, and legs feeling like rubber bands, I didn't stop moving until I could safely lean up against the first sturdy thing I encountered—the casket.

"Am I going crazy? Am I having a heart attack or something?" I asked the resident of the casket. Thankfully, he didn't reply.

I found the strength to pull myself together and went about my business of cleaning the chapel, all the while feeling as if I was being watched and not the only one in the room. The air conditioner kicked in several times as I bent over pews to collect used tissues or stooped near the casket to pick up flower petals. Each time it did, I jumped and grew impatient with myself, so I cranked the thermostat up to a higher temperature to stop the unit from kicking in as often. That was a mistake. The chapel, which had been my sanctuary, was now as quiet as the cooler room. I decided to deal with it, get my chapel cleaned, lower the temperature back down for the preservation of the flowers and the deceased, then shut things down and get the heck out of there. I stopped in my tracks upon hearing footsteps in the long interior hallway near the kitchen. I decided to think about it later and complete my chores.

It seemed like ages before I finished the chapel's cleaning. Once completed, I performed my last task in the chapel: turning off all the lights. I chose to start in the music room. As I entered the little room, located in the main lobby of the chapel, I bumped my knee on the piano bench. I looked down to check my stinging knee. There, on the bench, were the trash bags I had gotten out earlier in the day. I stared at them in disbelief, touching them to make sure they were real. I exited the music room and continued through the other areas of the chapel, turning off lights along the way, leaving only darkness behind. Lights in the lobby, restrooms, and main section of the chapel were all turned off. I remembered to readjust the thermostat before extinguishing the lights that illuminated the casket. With my hand on the dimmer switch, I slowly turned down the illumination on the face of an ordinary man who was so well loved in life and so deeply missed in death.

With quiet reverence, I exited the chapel and entered the mortuary's main hall. I pulled myself back into the here and now and continued on. Since Agnes had locked up the entire building and had done her own thorough check of the mortuary's interior rooms, I knew that another check wasn't necessary. I wanted out of there and knew that I had to walk by the cooler room to get to the alarm.

I took a deep breath, entered the interior hallway, and closed the first fire door that sealed off the employees' area from the rest of the mortuary. I turned, grabbed my purse and keys from the kitchen, and began my long walk down the hallway that seemed to have grown a lot longer and narrower than before. It was then that I noticed the door to the cooler room—it was closed! Not only was it closed, it was locked tight. I stared at the door in wonder, knowing that Agnes never closed or locked this door, when the sound of throat clearing happened again. I forced myself to walk calmly down the hallway to the alarm's keypad while closing the remaining two fire doors and switching off the last of the hall's many lights. I set the alarm with shaking hands and got the heck out of there for the night.

This series of events occurred in the cooler room a number of times. Each time, I became more familiar with the situation and calmer about whatever spirit or energy was causing this to happen.

One afternoon, prior to a family arriving for the visitation of their loved one, it started again. This time, I decided to speak to whomever or whatever was doing the mischief with the door and the lights. I felt a bit on the brave side, having thought about it for a few weeks and knowing that nothing had happened that was dangerous, just spooky. Noises couldn't harm me, the door never shut completely, and the lights never went out entirely.

So when the door started to close and the lights began to flicker, I put my hands on my hips, looked toward the door, and said, "Would you mind not doing that, please? It gives me the creeps." The lights stopped flickering and the door went back to the proper open position. I was impressed and a little bit shocked that this had worked and responded to the action, "So, looks like you can hear me. Thank you." I left the room and went on about my business.

Later that evening, while many folks still wandered the building, talking, drinking coffee, munching on snacks, and socializing, I went to the cooler room to get something. By this time I wasn't as fearful and just walked on in. The door began to close and the lights began to fade, so I said, "Oh, I'm sorry. I forgot to say hello. Hello. How are you?" Immediately, the door went back to the correct position, the lights came up, and even the atmosphere in the room changed.

The energy felt light and cheerful instead of cold and oppressive. From somewhere I got the nerve to approach the door. Where there had always been a chill was now warmth, not heat, just warmth in the air. When I placed my hand on the doorknob, it was warm to the touch, as if someone had just removed their hand from it. It was then that it struck me—ghosts were people, too!

I felt emotions of kindness and appreciation coming from the area near the door. The energy reached into my heart and touched my soul, causing my eyes to well up with tears; not from fear, but joy. This was truly a special moment. It appeared I had broken through and made contact. The energy had feelings, and those feelings spoke volumes. He was thankful; thankful for being acknowledged and thankful for being spoken to like the person he used to be. It was at that very moment that I knew I was definitely dealing with a spirit and this spirit had been male in life. I don't know how I knew, but I knew. I told him that I would be back, but had to return to my family. While walking down the hall, I heard a quiet laugh come from the cooler room. I asked myself if I had just made a friend and certainly hoped I had.

In the weeks that followed, he and I worked out a way to communicate. Even though I could hear him cough or laugh, I could not hear him speak. I would ask him a yes or no question and then leave the room. If the answer was yes, he was to shut the door all the way; if the answer was no, he was to leave the door fully open. Due to the tugging match we'd had a few weeks earlier, I was confident that he had the ability to shut the door or hold it open easily. The Doorman was fine with this system and even helped me have some harmless fun with a few of the funeral directors who liked to play tricks on me. I began to hear them ask, "What's up with that door lately?" in confusion as I quietly giggled at our spectral secret, hoping my new friend giggled as well. We had fun.

Over time I found out that this spirit had been a doorman at a posh hotel in the area several decades before. He had died young and was waiting for his wife, the love of his life, to come through the funeral home. He let me know that her time was coming soon and he would not cross over until she arrived. Knowing what awaited them both on the other side, he did not want to experience one moment of that beauty without her. Being immensely patient, he just wanted to continue being the Doorman until they could both cross over together.

Apparently, the Doorman appreciated the conversation, recognition, and acceptance that I gave; plus he was a touch of a romantic. I began to find single red carnations on top of the box of trash bags. I asked Agnes if she knew anything about these flowers, but she didn't. She and I noticed that they only showed up in the evenings after everyone else had left, and they only appeared after she'd gotten her trash bags. This was too eerie and spooky for Agnes, so she avoided saying anything when the flowers appeared while she was on duty. Some evenings, when I worked alone, they appeared at anytime or in other places. I found them on my purse or inside the back door lying next to the alarm's keypad at the end of the long interior hallway, in my car on the dashboard or on the wash basin of the employee's restroom. Agnes never asked if they showed up on nights she wasn't there. I don't think she wanted to know.

I asked the Doorman if he was the one leaving the red carnations. He answered yes by gently closing the door, but refused to answer or chose to ignore any other questions about them. The only question I got an answer to was, "Will I someday know the answers to all of my silly questions to you?" The answer was a resounding yes. The door practically slammed shut.

Unfortunately, I had to leave Serenity Shores. I needed to further my education and could not perform some of the needed requirements for my degree at that mortuary. After more than two years of working there, Serenity Shores had become like a second home to me. I was heartbroken at the thought of leaving. Prior to moving on, I took one of my co-workers into my confidence and explained the situation with the Doorman as well as with several other spirits that I had met along the way. She was thrilled, swore herself to secrecy, and informed me that she believed in spirits and life after death as well. She let me know she had felt someone around the cooler room door all along and had tried to communicate with him, too.

I informed the Doorman, along with the other spirits, that I would be leaving and that my colleague would be talking with them. To my surprise, they already knew; they knew about her as well and some were anxious to be in contact with her. This made me feel a little better even though I felt sad to leave my Doorman friend especially. I knew that he would be all right, though. After all, he did have a purpose and a reason for being there.

Long after leaving Serenity Shores and shortly after having to leave the business due to my physical health, I began having heartwarming and beautiful dreams about a man in a uniform, alone, walking on a cloud. His uniform was that of a doorman. He wore a long, beige coat that went to his knees with a black collar and cuffs, black slacks with satin trim along the outside of his legs, white gloves upon his hands, and a black top hat. He was quite dapper.

Then the dreams changed into two people walking on separate clouds. The man in the dream still had on the same uniform, and the other person was a beautiful woman in a flowing white gown that shimmered with light. The man and woman could see each other but not quite touch across the separation of the clouds. In each of these dreams, though, the clouds got closer and closer to one another.

One afternoon, after having many of these dreams, my co-worker from Serenity Shores phoned; she was very excited. She informed me that the night before, during a visitation, the power went out in the entire funeral home. When the lights came back on, all was fine except for one stand of carnations—red carnations. They had completely fallen apart. One red carnation remained intact, and some-how, during the power outage, it had been placed into the hands of the woman in the casket. The family told my co-worker that red carnations were their mother's favorite flowers. Their father, who had passed many years earlier, had given her one red carnation for times when they had to be apart, often placing it in her hand while she slept. When my colleague left the funeral home that night, on her purse she also found one red carnation.

The night she spoke of, when all this happened at the funeral home and before she called, I'd had the dream of the two people once again. They were now on the same cloud and walking together, hand in hand, into a mass of beautiful fluffy clouds. They turned as they walked and waved at me; in the woman's right hand was a red carnation.

After I hung up the phone, I went out to get my mail and there, just outside my front door, lay one perfect red carnation.

My former co-worker later told me the door doesn't move any longer. The Doorman told me I would know. She and I both know that our comical friend, the Doorman, finally met with his lady faire and is now together with her, forever, on the other side. May they both rest in peace and have great fun doing it.

Interesting note: As I wrote this account, a smell of perfume entered my room. It was a pleasant smell, not overpowering, and made me feel comfortable. I didn't know the scent, and still don't, but I know I liked it and found it comforting. I believe I was being visited by a spirit as I wrote.

CHAPTER 2

CHARLIE

Some psychologists say the most common phobia is that of public speaking. Morticians often find themselves speaking in front of gatherings, both large and small, so classes in communication are part of the required curriculum for a mortuary science degree. Whether we address a group in reference to the final viewing and closing procedure, or if we need to write and deliver a eulogy for someone we've never met, as funeral personnel we know we will be required to speak to the public. This makes us a little nervous sometimes, but we persevere.

No matter how many times someone speaks publicly, a touch of butterflies upon approaching the microphone is normal. For some people, however, speaking into a microphone is often their preferred manner of communication, even after death.

That happened to be the case with a spirit named Charlie.

I had been working at Serenity Shores Mortuary for more than a year when I first began to hear a voice in the smallest of the mortuary's many chapels. The white brick walls, thick carpet, heavy internal fire doors, and solid oak carved outer doors made the room soundproof. This chapel is so small, intimate, and private that people have commented on it feeling like a tomb.

Late one night, after the conclusion of four services and visitations, I was cleaning and preparing the building for the next day's dead. Jim, an associate of mine, was performing the same duties in one of the parlors located down the main hallway, near the front lobby.

As I walked from the largest of the chapels toward the employee back hall, I passed by the open interior fire door of the tiny chapel. As I did, I heard a whispering male voice coming from inside the chapel. I immediately thought that Jim had gone in there to clean and needed some assistance. I called out to him and asked if he could repeat what he'd just said. Upon entering the room, I saw that the only light available came in through the windows from the floodlights outside. I turned on the interior lights, looked around the room, and saw no one, but called out to Jim anyway. There was no reply so I walked through the tiny room to make sure he wasn't under a pew or in the flower niches near where the casket sits.

I saw that the heat was off, the room was completely clean, and there wasn't a casket there for any service the next day; there was also no Jim. As he stood six foot four in his stocking feet, there was no way I could have missed him. I thought I was hearing things, maybe ringing in my ears caused by one of the noisy services earlier. Turning off all the lights, I left the chapel, and didn't think much more about it.

Jim and I completed our tasks of cleaning and straightening the parlors and other chapels, bringing in the loaded caskets, and positioning the floral arrangements for the next morning's services. While I put the final touches to the folds of velvet encircling the base of a bier I asked Jim if he'd been in the tiny chapel earlier. He said he hadn't and asked if I, too, had heard whispering sounds coming from the room; he'd been hearing it all evening. His opinion was that we heard voices out of that space because we had had so much noise going on all over the building and the tiny chapel was the only room that was quiet. I accepted his explanation but thought it interesting that he had also heard the whispering and felt the need to explain it.

Jim and I weren't the only ones who heard whispering coming from the humble little chapel. On various occasions, my co-workers asked if I had been in there and whispering oddly. One evening, I was managing a quietly subdued private viewing in one of the larger parlors down the hall from the whispering chapel. Few people showed up to pay their last respects, but at least the family members were in attendance. With little to do and no other services in the building, the night dragged on. The visitors in the parlor milled about comfortably and didn't need much attention, which made me think it would be a great time to investigate the tiny chapel. I figured I could easily run down the hall and tend to the needs of the family, if they needed me.

Even though the mood of the visitors in the parlor was somber, there were still the sounds of quiet conversation and soothing music drifting down the hall as I approached the open chapel's fire door. When I walked through the doorway, however, the parlor sounds vanished as if someone had shut the door on a tomb. The air in the room was oddly still and very peaceful. I felt as if I was enveloped in total calm, peace, and solitude. What at first was a little shocking quickly became overwhelmingly comforting. If I had wanted to, I could have curled up and taken a wonderful nap. I began to feel intoxicated and knew that this feeling could not be allowed to progress.

I shook off the euphoria that was overtaking me and turned on the lights. I began my investigation by searching for anything that could allow sound from elsewhere to filter into the room. I looked for loose air vents and electrical sockets that could vibrate. I checked the wiring in the flower niches as well as the seal around the flower exit door, which we used to take floral arrangements out to the vans that transported them to the cemetery. I looked under the pews, inside flower stands, and around the dais that housed the microphone. I checked the tiny music room and found the power to the equipment was off. As I found nothing to reveal the cause of the whisper, I went back to the family in the parlor. They were great to attend to and the easiest one I'd taken care of in weeks.

The next night, I had another small, intimate group present for a viewing of their loved one in the tiny chapel. Before they arrived, I sat quietly in the chapel, taking a moment to gather my thoughts. I went through the checklist in my head to make sure all was ready for the evening: coffee, flowers, memorial print material, cookies, and the deceased. All was perfect, so I could now sit for a few moments to center myself while taking a long-needed deep breath. It was then that I heard the whispering start up ever so slightly.

I came to immediate attention while my ears searched for whatever they could pick up. I tried to find the direction the whispering was coming from and began feeling the comfort of the night before. I had to filter the sound as noise in the rest of the building from the staff drifted into the room. I wondered if I was hearing things, but the whispering persisted. Looking for the source all around the room, I finally discerned that the whispering was coming out of the speakers.

I thought maybe an audio signal from a radio nearby was causing the input, so I checked the microphone and speaker connections. I checked inside the sound booth to see if something there was sending sound across and out from the speakers. All I found was the sound equipment powered down. I walked into the center of the chapel and stopped in the aisle between the rows of pews.

I scratched my head and said out loud, "This sure is funny. It's like someone's actually talking into the mike."

A louder whisper now came through the speakers and clearly stated, "I am!"

I slowly turned toward the microphone on the dais; I saw nothing. I cautiously asked, "Is there someone there?"

"Yesss," the whisper replied.

"Are you spirit?" I asked.

"Yesss," it calmly answered. I was freaked out and could hear my heart beating in my chest, but at the same time I thought this was wonderful. I was able to speak with a spirit. I realized I had to be careful speaking out loud in the room as anyone from the office could walk by and wonder who I was talking to, so I spoke in a whispered tone also.

"If I speak like this, can you still hear me?" I whispered.

The answer came back, "Yesss."

"Well, good," I said, "then I can talk to you and nobody should hear."

The voice then said, a little louder this time, "Watch out!" One of the office staff suddenly flounced into the room to let me know she was going home for the night. She had heard voices in the chapel and asked who I'd been talking to. I made up something quick for a cover and told her I was going over some information for a report I was working on at school. She said that was good, as she was beginning to wonder if I was losing it, with working late nights in the funeral home alone and all.

"Sorting out information verbally is always a good thing," she told me. I said thanks and bid her a good evening.

I followed her out of the chapel and checked to make sure I was the only living body left in the building. When I re-entered the tiny chapel, I leaned up against one of the pews in an oh-boy-that-was-a-close-one stance. I heard the voice giggle and say "Good one!"

I looked up at the speaker and said, "Thanks, I needed that."

Up until the time the family arrived, I chatted with the voice whom I now knew was male. I found out his name was Charlie, and when he had died his body had lain in state in our funeral home. He liked it there and had decided to hang out. I spoke to him about crossing over and asked him about going into the light. He let me know firmly that not all spirits are ready to go into the light; they may have unfinished business or want to observe for a while. Going into the light isn't an option for some spirits and it can be traumatic when a well-intentioned healer or medium forces them across, especially if they're not creating havoc or hurting anyone. While some go through a learning process to obtain higher enlightenment before heading across, others linger to atone for something they've done in the life they've lost.

When the family arrived, I went into the chapel's sound room to adjust the microphone and music for the evening. I had forgotten that the system was completely powered down, so I had a good laugh at myself while checking the power connections and sound levels. After putting on restful harp music, I checked on the family and found that all was well. I turned around at the wooden doorway leading into the tiny chapel and leaned on the doorjamb with my arms folded and knowingly looked toward the microphone on the dais with a smile on my face. I wondered if Charlie was watching from somewhere in the room. I also wondered what the family would think if they knew our sound system worked, while turned off, for one special spirit who whispers into microphones.

From time to time, Charlie and I continued our chats. He gave me a lot of insight into the world of spirit and was often there to listen to my problems as well as support and comfort me if I was feeling blue. Unfortunately, Charlie didn't like to talk about himself very much. But he loved to listen and teach, and sometimes gave great advice.

Our conversations had to come to an end, though, when I moved on to another mortuary. I informed a co-worker about Charlie just as I had with the Doorman. She still works at Serenity Shores and calls me with updates. She tells me that the sound system, including the speakers and the microphone, have all been rewired, remodeled, and upgraded, but Charlie still listens and speaks to her. She is happy that someone there can chat with her when things get stressful.

She phoned recently to let me know Charlie was still there, along with some of the others, and she finds him to be helpful to her when she has problems. Yes, Charlie is a great listener with fabulous insight. We don't know anything else about him; he still doesn't like to talk about himself. My co-worker feels that he's an angel. Maybe that's what Charlie really is: an angel who has a way with a public address system.

CHAPTER 3

SISTER MARY

Many times we hear of someone who courageously runs into a burning building or jumps into an ice-laden river to save another. Once in a while these selfless individuals are caught on video performing their terrifying and heroic acts of bravery. These are people we would like to get to know. But often they are nowhere to be found when it comes time to give them our heartfelt thanks and public gratitude. We stare at our television sets and wonder if an angel or spirit had come to help. We may find ourselves talking about whether or not things like this can happen or how a spirit or angel can make itself so solid that it can lift a human or an animal.

Simply put, spirits can often fully manifest when there is a real need or sometimes just to give a warm hug. Whether they are a spirit returned from the dead or an angel from on high, when they manifest, we may not know it unless we see that same one over and over again.

Early in my career, I was blessed to meet a sweet lady who was unlike any other. I met her for the first time during the visitation for a child. The family was lost, bereaved, and full of the understandable question of "Why?" The child had not been on this earth for long yet was loved by so many people, young and old alike. Many who attended tried to console and calm the child's young parents and siblings, but with all of the love in the world with them in that chapel, they still couldn't be soothed, at least not until the sweet, elderly lady walked into the scene.

The lobby to the chapel was packed with several dozen people. Quietly and unassumingly, a tiny, elderly woman who was five feet tall and wearing the modern nun's habit of shorter skirt, shoulder-length veil, and sensible shoes entered the lobby through the main doors. Among the throng of people, I noticed her right away.

She was having trouble getting through the crowd, and that's when I stepped in. I worked my way over to her and asked, "May I help you, Sister?"

"Oh, that would be very kind of you, Mariah," she answered rather breathlessly as she took my hand. She wanted to sign the guest book and get a memorial folder. Then she asked where the family was seated. I was about to escort her to the front of the chapel, through the mass of people, but when I turned to guide her, nearly everyone had left the area. I commented on this and her very jovial reply came back.

"That tends to happen when I'm around, dear. I'll see myself to the front, now. You just stay out here and do what you're needed to do. Thank you," she said with a humble, yet knowing, smile on her face as she gently patted my hand that I hadn't even realized she held in her own.

I observed this diminutive lady walk gracefully and determinedly up to the casket of the little girl. She stood by the child for quite some time and then, as if by magic, made her way through the throng of caring individuals surrounding the grieving family in the front pews. When she made her way to the two young parents, their attention was immediately on her; again, like magic. I observed the three of them sitting and speaking together. The other mourners seemed to know that the three needed to be left alone. It was beautiful to feel the change in the people all around as well as feel the tension in the room lift. Truly, a breath of fresh air flooded the room as this woman moved throughout.

Soon, the little nun walked out of the chapel and let me know she was leaving.

"Well, my work here is done. See you next time, Mariah," she stated as she took my hand and gave it another little pat. I asked for her name and she stated, "Why, Sister Mary, of course." My only response was a quiet thank you, even though I was wondering which church she was affiliated with. She walked out of the building but not before turning back around and, as if reading my mind, answered the silent question rambling around in my head.

"I'm from Our Lady of Angelic Devotion, dear," she said while wearing that same humble, yet knowing, smile on her wonderfully angelic face. I thanked her and we parted company.

After all had left the building and I was in my cleanup process, it hit me. "Hey! Wait a minute. How'd she know I wanted to ask her which church she belonged to? And another thing—how in the heck did she know my name?" I do not wear a nametag and I had not mentioned my name to her, nor had I ever met her before. I stood next to the casket containing the body of a beautiful child whose life had ended too soon and knew that we both had the honor of meeting someone who was, indeed, very special—I just didn't yet realize how special.

Sister Mary showed up often. She came to all visitations, services, and burials for deceased children whether they were Catholic or not. She always had a special demeanor with the families, as well as with anyone else who was particularly distraught, lost, or hurting. A dose of Sister Mary was all people seemed to need to help them with their bereavement. Everyone appreciated the actions of the little nun, and many asked where this wonderful little lady had come from. I told them the only things I knew about her— her name and the name of her church.

One early evening, my co-worker and friend Agnes worked a visitation for a child and asked if I thought the spooky little nun would show up that evening. I said I certainly hoped so since she had such a good effect on people. Agnes disagreed and said Sister Mary gave her the creeps. She didn't know why, as she really wanted to like the little nun, but for some reason, she just couldn't. I shook my head while wondering how this could be.

I went on about my business seeing to the needs of the family I was in charge of when Agnes ran into my area and let me know that Sister Mary had arrived.

"What should I do?" she asked frantically.

I told her to let her do her thing; she never hurts anyone, and always leaves the family in a better frame of mind than they were before.

"Yeah, but this family isn't Catholic! They don't believe in anything. They even had me take the cross off the wall. I think they're offended!" she replied in a slight panic.

I somehow knew that all would be fine. I looked at Agnes with what I hoped was a knowing look that would make her feel better and stated, "Believe me. Everything will be just fine. It'll all work out."

"But, these ..." she started. I didn't let her finish as I knew that she had to get back and see for herself.

In the meantime, the visitors came and went for the viewing I was attending to. A large, black SUV pulled into the parking lot containing four women whom I noticed because they looked to be wearing veils. When they entered my chapel, I saw that their veils were the same as Sister Mary's. As a unit, the nuns signed the guest book, took their prayer cards, and moved down the aisle toward the casket with precision that would put the navy's Blue Angels to shame.

When I saw the women relaxing in the back pews and chatting among themselves, I quietly approached them. I inquired if they were from Our Lady of Angelic Devotion. When they said they were, I let them know that one of their dear Sisters was in the next chapel helping out another family. They looked at each other quizzically, then asked her name and what she looked like.

As I answered their questions, one of them jumped up and asked, "Is it a child?"

I answered in the affirmative and she told the eldest nun, "Mother, I'll go." Reverend Mother nodded, turned to me and stated, "Please, take Sister Margaret over there to see her. I promise she won't intrude."

At which point, Sister Margaret energetically pled her case, "Yes, I promise, I won't intrude at all. I just have to see her, please."

My family was doing fine, so I escorted Sister Margaret across the yard to the parlor. Agnes was standing calmly in the hallway outside the parlor with a serene look on her face. I introduced Sister Margaret to Agnes and let my now amazingly calm friend know that she wanted to see Sister Mary and would not intrude. Her blissfully calm hand motioned toward the inner area where we could see Sister Mary.

We saw her surrounded by people, young and old alike, in all manner of dress, hanging on her every word. I asked Sister Margaret if she would like to be escorted in. It was at this moment that I noticed she had gone ghostly pale and her mouth was slack as a tear moved down her careworn cheek. Being concerned for this gentle woman, I asked if she was all right and could I do anything for her.

"No, my dear, you've already done it. I thank you," she answered as if in a daze while catching her breath to stifle a sob. She quietly motioned that she wanted to return to the other chapel.

As we crossed the yard leading back to my chapel, we saw the other nuns had left the building and were now standing together in the circular driveway. They signaled for us to come over to them. As we approached, I saw that they were greatly anticipating any information Sister Margaret was ready to share. I began to head back into my chapel, but was immediately grabbed on the arm by the very firm yet gentle, vise-like grip of Reverend Mother.

I was pulled into the group and saw that Sister Margaret was trying very hard to speak through her confusion and shock. She finally took a well-needed deep breath and said simply, "Our dear old friend, our Sister, Mary, is in there." The Sisters, as one, gasped in awe and amazement, then blessed themselves with the sign of the cross. Reverend Mother put her hand to her mouth and asked Sister Margaret if she was certain, to which she nodded in the affirmative.

The nuns now turned their full attention to me and asked many things about their friend. I answered their questions to the best of my ability and then saw Agnes come out of her parlor. She still had a look of serenity about her.

"Did you see her?" Agnes asked us. "She just left; walked right by you all." We had seen no one walk by us. Agnes told us how Sister Mary calmed everyone in the room and took her time in speaking with each of them. How she seemed to take control with the most gentle of hands. Then Agnes told us of how kind, gentle, and reassuring the good Sister had been to her. Sister Mary had made her feel better than she had felt in years. This was odd for Agnes to admit, as she rarely spoke of her feelings. The nuns were now greatly moved and quietly pulled handkerchiefs from their sleeves to wipe their silent tears.

When Agnes left, the Sisters asked my name. Reverend Mother gently took my hand, looked at me kindly with her tear-stained eyes, and said, "Mariah, Sister Mary loved children. She was always so good with their families and made everyone in the room feel her love and kindness. She never knew a stranger."

"You're speaking in the past tense, Sister," I politely pointed out.

"I know," she stated. "You see, Sister Mary was taken from us accidentally when she was trying to help a child. She was hit by a car several years ago. We've heard rumors that she had somehow returned and now we've seen it for ourselves. Her love made so many people calm and so happy. Sometimes it made them uncomfortable, too, but everything always seemed to work out around her." She giggled while a few tears gently moved down her cheek. "That woman's love was equaled by few. We're glad it didn't die with her."

I stood awestruck, not knowing what to say. I forced myself to shake it off and return to my family in the chapel. As I entered my chapel, I turned to watch the nuns in the black SUV exit the parking lot. I thought to myself, "I'm glad her love didn't die, too. I guess that proves what I've always known—love never dies."

These occurrences with Sister Mary all took place at Serenity Shores Mortuary. She was one of the spirits I was afraid I would never have the chance to meet again when I moved on to further my education. When I went to work at my next funeral home, Sherwood Mortuary and Cremation Service, one of the first cases I had complete charge over was that of a beautiful young girl who had passed due to a terminal illness. This young lady had the pride and determination to plan her own funeral. She took the time to learn about embalming and decide not to have that done, as well as deciding how she was to be dressed, which of her favorite cosmetics were to be used on her face, along with how, and what music was to play. She also wanted the nun who had visited her in the hospital to be there.

I worked incessantly trying to see to the final wishes of this brave young girl. But I could not locate the nun who had visited her. I called hospital staff and administrators; I even spoke with the medical examiner and morgue attendants. I couldn't find that woman. I had accomplished everything on the list but felt like I had failed her due to not being able to complete this one task. The family compassionately understood, which just made me feel worse.

On the evening of her public visitation and service, the young girl's friends set up the chapel with her favorite things exactly as she wished. Her family was in a private viewing room for their time alone with their beloved daughter. The weather outside was horrible—cold, wet, rainy, and windy, with a lot of lightning.

As I made my way from the private viewing room, through the L-shaped lobby entrance of the building toward the chapel, I heard a loud crack of thunder and saw a bright flash of lightning. The wind had picked up violently, blowing the swinging glass entry doors wide open. As I had my back to them when the lightning hit, I ducked. When I turned around, there, standing in the open doorway between the two glass doors was a diminutive woman dressed well against the storm. She wore a yellow rain slicker, gray rain boots, a blue scarf wrapped around her neck, and a red rain hat covering her head. Very calmly she stood on the floor mat and shook out her Day-Glo green umbrella. She turned and closed the two glass doors as I moved toward her.

"Oh, my goodness, Mariah, this is a blustery night, isn't it?" she breathlessly commented. I knew that voice. As she turned while taking off her rain hat and scarf, I saw the black fabric of a nun's veil gently fall upon her neck. I realized I was once again looking upon Sister Mary. I was speechless and elated.

"I heard through the grapevine that you've been looking for me," she said calmly and quietly while taking off her outer garments. "I'm a little difficult to find, but I'll always be around when I'm needed. Now, here are my things. Could you please show me to the family?"

I was beside myself and at a loss for words.

Sister Mary handed me her outer garments and umbrella, which I placed in the clergy room next to the lobby. She took my hand as she had done before, and we walked toward the private viewing lounge. Immediately, the family recognized the woman and welcomed her with open arms and warm feelings. As I quietly closed the door to the room, Sister Mary told me to be sure I had lots of tissues in the chapel. There were going to be a lot of people there, she said, and they would be arriving shortly.

This all started a little past five o'clock in the evening after everyone I worked with at Sherwood had gone home for the evening. Sister Mary arrived about half past five and stayed with the family for more than an hour. During this time, people arrived for the public portion of the evening commencing at seven, but not nearly as many as I would have liked. Sister Mary called me into the private lounge and let me know that it *was time*. The family nodded in agreement.

I solemnly and reverently approached the casket containing the young girl. Instead of a floral casket spray, the family had set her favorite stuffed animals at the foot of the casket. Her younger siblings lovingly took these precious plushies from my hands as I removed them to completely close the casket for the last time. As I slowly lowered the lid of her casket, Sister Mary stood with the family. I could hear her uttering a small and quiet prayer, just as I was doing.

As I began to guide the casket out of the lounge toward the viewing chapel, Sister Mary asked to take the head of the casket while I guided the foot end. I knew the head portion of the casket would be secure in this tiny woman's blessed hands. The girl's family followed behind as we began our quiet procession. When I opened the door of the private lounge, I saw that the entire lobby was now full of people. I was amazed at how many people had arrived in the short time I had been in the private lounge.

As we moved through the lobby and into the chapel, I noticed that the storm had stopped and things were quiet outside as well as inside. I uttered a quiet thank you for the blessings that this evening had brought, while solemnly moving the casket into the chapel and aligning it near the front dais.

Sister Mary and I secured the casket in place by seven o'clock; she knew what she was doing, including being certain that the wheels of the church cot were in perfect alignment so that the casket wouldn't tip if leaned upon. I proceeded to leave the family and visitors in the loving and capable hands of Sister Mary as they preferred to run this service themselves.

Just before nine o'clock, Sister Mary left the chapel and walked out the front door to check the weather. She came back in, walked into the clergy room, and donned her rain gear. I went in to assist, but she let me know she was fine.

A minute later, with red rain hat on head and Day-Glo green umbrella in hand, she told me, "I'll always be around when I'm needed; now, don't you ever forget that."

She once again took my hand, gave it a little pat, and let go. With a tiny smile on her face and a knowing twinkle in her eye, she turned and headed toward the door.

"Don't worry about any of these fine people," she told me before opening the swinging glass door. "They'll all make it home safely, just like you will. The weather will hold. Have a good day off tomorrow, dear." She turned and briskly walked down the cement sidewalk. As she moved so quickly, I was worried that she would slip on the damp pavement and ran out of the building to make sure she made it to her car all right. She was nowhere to be seen and had just disappeared.

When I walked back in, that's when it hit me. I wondered how she knew that I had the next day off.

The weather did hold. Everyone made it home safely. As I was the last to leave, I can safely assume that I was also the last to get home. As I pulled into my garage, the storm began again with all the fury that it had wielded earlier.

I rest assured, knowing that should anyone have the unfortunate cause to attend the funeral of a child and a little nun walks in with big, grey eyes wearing sensible shoes, they shouldn't be afraid to approach her and ask her name. Their life will never be the same.

CHAPTER 4

THE KNOWING GUARDIAN

I'm afraid of the dark. I have been ever since I was a small child and was forced to go to bed long before anyone else in the house. I hated being in a darkened room, especially if I was alone. I told people there were weird things, creepy stuff, and dead people in the dark. Most folks wouldn't listen. They'd laugh and tell me that nothing is in the dark that wasn't there in the light.

One day, when I was four years old, after much complaining on my part about what I had seen in the dark, my family sat me down. They admitted that, even though we could all see spirits and sometimes even talk to them, we should not let other people know. This didn't help me overcome my fear of the dark. Even at a young age, I knew the people I saw in the dark had something in common. They were all dead. I didn't know how, I didn't know why, I just knew that they were dead. My family could turn on all the nightlights they wanted; that didn't change the fact that most of the energies in the dark, the things that I heard go bump in the night, were dead. This really used to bother me.

As a funeral attendant at Serenity Shores Mortuary, I was often the last one to leave at night and often worked alone in the dark building. After tending to my regular duties, I would take a final peek at the deceased to make sure they were safe and tucked in for the night. Then, my final responsibility was to inspect the entire funeral home, darkened room by darkened room, and make sure no living person had decided to hide in the building. When all was clear, I locked up the mortuary and set the alarm. I did all this even though I was, and am, very afraid of the dark.

The first time I was completely alone at Serenity Shores was the first time I'd ever been left alone in a funeral home. I was nervous and afraid that someone or something was going to jump out at me. Every night, I worked hard to shake this silly feeling. I did fairly well at conquering this fear until late one night when I needed to stay much later than usual.

The family I was taking care of had a difficult time saying their final good-byes to their loved one. The handsome deceased gentleman was in an elegant casket in the large chapel on the southernmost end of the mortuary. Most visitations ended by nine; this one had gone on past ten. The lights were on in the chapel and the adjoining corridors and halls, so I wasn't nervous. At least I wasn't until the last person finally left for the night.

At that point, I locked and bolted the large, oak double doors of the chapel. I had already cleaned the restrooms and emptied the trash, turned off the music, and set the furnace's thermostat for the night. All was complete, I felt pretty good, and I could now head home—or so I thought until I turned around after taking my hands off the now secured doors.

Upon turning around, I had the sudden feeling of not being alone. I had the distinct feeling of being stared at, which made my skin crawl. The hair on the back of my neck began to rise and the room had gone cold—far too cold. Even with the heat set low for the night, a slight breeze came from somewhere. While shivering, I checked the rooms off the lobby—the restrooms, clergy room, and music room—and found them all to be empty. I forced myself to turn off the lights in the chapel's lobby all the while knowing I wasn't alone.

I took the long walk down the aisle of the chapel approaching the deceased in the casket. I kept my eyes focused upon the casket thinking that the resident was about to do something; but thankfully, nothing moved. I could now see my breath the closer I moved toward the casket; the area was like walking into a freezer. As I gazed into the casket, praying that the dead man wouldn't move, I turned my head in the direction of the emergency exit doors to the left of the casket. I needed to make sure they were locked securely and saw that one of them was open about three inches.

"That explains it," I chuckled, "a bit of night breeze. I knew there was a logical explanation for this." I locked and bolted this door, too.

Having gotten over my little fright, I felt a little cocky as I turned off the lights in the chapel—never thinking once about the dark that engulfed me as I did so—and made my way into the connecting corridor leading into the long employee hallway, back door, and alarm keypad. I paused in the dark corridor to do a mental check on everything. With pitch dark behind me and blinding light in front of me, I completed my mental checklist with confidence and moved forward.

I didn't feel the least bit twitchy as I bolted the three fire doors that separated different sections of the back hallway and turned off each section's lights. These sections, along with their heavy, insulated steel, bolted doors, isolated the dressing room, cooler room, and prep room in case of fire. With all the lights off, only the light from a red security lamp glowed like flames under the last locked fire door.

I removed the keys from my purse so that once the alarm was set I could exit and lock the back door within the required forty-five seconds. I looked up at the alarm status lights, with my thumb positioned over the keypad, when I saw them switch from green-for-go to red-for-open. I stared at the tiny red light.

"Hey, I locked everything, I shut everything. Wait a minute …" went through my head as I began to feel my heart pound. I slowly turned my head to look down the completely darkened hall and into the smothering blackness. I saw only the flame-red security light beckon menacingly from under the door. I knew that a door had been opened as I stood there alone in the dark.

"Did I miss someone hiding under one of the pews?" I quietly asked. I shut my mouth hoping I wouldn't receive an answer out of the dark. Time stood still. What took only a few seconds seemed like forever. I went into a frozen state, feeling if I stayed quiet, it would go away.

I knew that I had to go back, unlock doors that I'd locked and traverse darkened areas. My heart pounded in my ears, I heard every breath I took, and each step I took reverberated against the hard walls. As I approached the first fire door, I paused with my hand on the lock and wondered if I should run outside, call the police and my husband, then just sit in the car with the doors locked and radio turned up. That would have been the smart thing to do. That's what most people would have done. "Chicken!" I called myself as I decided to check it out on my own, be alert, and keep my pepper spray in my hand just in case.

I unlocked the first fire door and fumbled for the light. A red glow from the security light flooded through the door until I found the switch. I moved through each of the three fire areas of the back hall, all the while dropping keys and fumbling for lights. For some reason, during all of the fumbling and dropping, I felt drawn toward the chapel I had just left, the one with the emergency door near the casket where I had laughed at myself earlier. I wasn't laughing now since that's where I knew I had to go.

I crossed the dark central corridor leading into the chapel's secluded family area. I closed my eyes as I entered the pitch black room and fumbled for the light switch. Once located, I broke a nail as I clawed for the light. With the safety of the light, I knew that I'd been holding my breath; my throat had tightened for a scream. I took a deep breath and surveyed the room and saw nothing.

With wobbly knees, I forced my now-shaking body forward into the darkened chapel, trying to remain calm as I made my way to the foot of the casket and the light switch nearby. With eyes wide open, I felt for the switch on the wall while never taking my eyes off of the casket. I threw on the switch for all the lights to illuminate the room, praying that the dead man wasn't sitting up in his casket, pointing a finger at me. With the flood of light, I focused upon the open casket. He was resting just as I'd left him; stressed laughter made its way out of my throat. While patting my hand on the foot of the casket, I uttered words of thankful praise to every holy being that I'd ever known, along with a few I'd only read about, while tears filled my eyes.

I breathed a sigh of relief after thanking my maker and was relieved until I felt the chill and breeze of earlier. My attention was drawn to the door left of the casket once again. I became aware of what I did not want to see. The door stood open several inches.

Knowing I had secured that very door just a few minutes earlier, I gathered my courage, slowly approached the door, and shut it again. I checked it twice, threw my weight against it, and put all to rights just as before. I moved quickly this time, determinedly walking with my head down and the tension rising within me; stress keeping the screams, tears, and other bodily fluids inside. I kept my head down just in case something was off to the side that I didn't want to see and made certain my feet were making contact with the floor.

I went through the same routine down that long back hall, bolting each fire door again, and checking the red security lights. I made my way to the alarm keypad once again, now counting each step I made and each breath I took. I could hear my voice pulling at the back of my throat just wanting to let out a scream. My jaw ached as little whimpers made their way through the fear. I just wanted out of there.

Approaching the alarm keypad once again, keys at the ready, hallways dark, and fire doors locked, I aimed my thumb at the keypad to punch in the code. Again, the lights switched from the safety of green to the alert of red as I stared at the keypad. This time my fear and panic changed; I became filled with annoyance and unbridled anger.

I made a fist, set my jaw, and tossed my purse onto the hard linoleum floor. I spoke loudly to whatever was playing games with me. "Now, you knock this off. I'm getting tired of this. I wanna go home. It's late, and I haven't eaten yet." With this I uttered a few four-letter words and knew right where to go. Dark or no dark, light or no light, I moved through fire doors, hallway, and darkened corridor with blind determination. I didn't flinch this time or drop my keys. Shaking was out of the question and breathing was fine.

As I made my way into the chapel, I stomped directly to the door next to the casket with only the illumination from a small set of lights in the little family area. The door was in the same position, open about an inch, with a slight breeze blowing in. I again secured it and didn't care one bit about the dark or the deceased. To me, at that time, the dark was only the dark and the deceased wasn't going anywhere until tomorrow. I knew a spirit was playing with that door; playing and having fun. But this time I was too angry, too hungry, and too tired to care. I stood in the chapel and spoke into the darkness as if speaking to a naughty child.

"Okay!" I said with my hands on my hips. "You've had your fun. Now will you let me go home? Oh, and by the way, you need to stay here. Got it?" I really wasn't expecting an answer, but I heard a loud bang as if someone had hit their hand on the wooden clergy dais two feet away from me.

I ran out of the building and later envisioned my feet moving like a cartoon exiting a scene quickly but not getting traction. I made sure to turn off and lock up everything as I'd done before. The keypad was green for go and it stayed that way. I set the alarm, walked out, and locked the back door. I walked quickly to my car and peeled out of the parking lot.

About a mile from my house, traffic was at a dead stop. The red and blue lights of police vehicles were ahead, along with several rescue vehicles. I focused on the mass of organized chaos and saw the officers encircling a bad car wreck with fatalities. I saw more than one tarp covering indistinguishable lumps of matter that had been living, breathing people just a short time earlier. As I waited for the traffic to be re-directed, I saw a police officer I knew who had visited the funeral home. I flagged him over and asked about the accident. He brought his head down to my window level and quietly said, "Yep, this is a bad one. Three people dead. Be glad you weren't on this section of road twenty minutes ago. You'd have been in it, too."

I became numb and knew the officer was right. It hit me like a ton of bricks. Had it not been for the door spirit, I would have been driving in that area at the time of the accident. That could have been me under one of those tarps. Had I gone out to my car and called for help, that could have been someone I loved mangled in that mess. I was beside myself in awe of the reality of what had transpired earlier and the now revealed reason behind it. I was forced to delay my trip home to avoid this tragedy. I had been protected.

I put my car in park knowing that it would be a minute or two before traffic would be allowed to divert around the scene. I allowed myself the luxury of taking a look over my shoulder, back toward the direction of the funeral home. The up-and-down stress of the last thirty minutes took its toll; I could no longer control my emotions or hold back the tears. I now knew—I now understood. The spirit hadn't been playing with me; he'd been protecting and guarding me, watching and keeping me safe from harm. The spirit knew.

I sobbed uncontrollably, catching my breath to let the tension release. Not only did the spirit make it so that I escaped the path of the Reaper, he made it so that I was forced to confront a lifelong fear. The strength of unselfish protection and thoughtfulness from someone dead gave me the courage to walk into the dark. At that moment, it also gave me the ability I needed to pull myself together and drive on as traffic began to move. For the first time in almost fifty years, I felt I had an ally in the dark. I laughed a bit as I drove on and realized that I had some apologies to make along with some thanks to give to a spirit near a door.

I didn't mention this spirit's name because I didn't know it until I'd gotten time to speak with Charlie's spirit to find out the name of the spirit in the southern chapel. His name was Henry and he often prevented people from getting on the road when something nasty was about to occur. I took each incident with a grain of salt and figured out ways to get my co-workers to sit and cool their jets for a few minutes until the keypad light stayed on green. I always knew that it would, and of course, it was always the same door in the same chapel that was the culprit.

Often, when the light gave the okay, I would stay behind with the excuse that I'd forgotten something. Everybody else would leave, but I would go into the southern chapel, say "Thank you, Henry," and then tap the wooden dais twice. As I walked away, I always got a tap-tap-tap in reply.

Good night, Henry, and thank you—tap, tap.

CHAPTER 5

THE HELPERS

When one least expects it, one can receive assistance from those who have passed on. Those who are here to help do so in some mundane ways while others are so over the top they can leave one wondering. Spirits have been known to lend a helping hand in ways that vary from bringing in a newspaper out of the rain to saving someone from drowning when their car crashes into a swimming pool. They may appear as a slight puff of smoke, a fully detailed and solid manifestation, or nothing at all. Their movements can range from slight and subtle to huge and outrageous.

While some people feel that spirits or ghosts are only malevolent in nature, I have found this not to be true, as most spirits are positive and helpful, even if they are a bit on the spooky side. It's the ones that create problems or simply just want to be noticed or acknowledged that get the bad rap. Fortunately, I've encountered not only the noisy and demonstrative spirits while working in funeral homes, but also the helpful souls as well.

Many mornings, I was the first to arrive early at the funeral home. At Serenity Shores, my normal daily routine was to enter the property from the eastern driveway so that I could do a full-on, visual security check of the parking lot and the building, then park in the back. It always gave me a warm feeling seeing the morning paper on our carpeted stoop as I drove in—kind of like I was coming home instead of just arriving to work.

I'd always be nervous when opening the funeral home's back door because I was afraid I'd set off the alarm or forget the security code. After successfully turning off the alarm, my next task was to go down the long employee hallway to start the day's first pot of coffee, then head toward the front door to bring in the newspaper.

Many times as I approached the large double-glass doors, I realized the paper was already inside the building and cool to the touch. The doors were locked tight and the alarm never tripped; access to the alarm keypad was nowhere near these front doors. I would attempt to slip the paper under or through the door to see if that was how the paper got inside; all to no avail. Finally, I would thank the spirit that did this chore for me, saving me the hassle of having to unlock, then re-lock, the front doors.

The same thing would happen with coffee carafes and boxes of tissues when I was the first to arrive at the funeral home—they wouldn't be there, then they would be. The spirits saved me some steps on more than one occasion, and

I sincerely appreciated it. When I knew a spirit was there, whether I felt them or caught their movement out of the corner of my eye, I always took a moment to thank them for their assistance.

Sometimes, I would find extra trash bags or bottles of water in my personal areas of the chapels I worked in. Several attendants also found these gifts set out for them. They would ask if I had something to do with it, to which I would truthfully answer no. Occasionally, a fellow attendant became unnerved by these actions so I would take credit to keep the peace. One afternoon, after taking the credit for a kindness I didn't do, I felt the need to apologize to the spirits. I did so while setting up for the evening's visitation in the tiny chapel.

"We know. We understand," came Charlie's voice in response, softly and clearly, over the loudspeaker. I jumped each and every time I heard his voice, but I felt better knowing the spirits knew and understood my plight.

Several co-workers, however, were terrified of the spirits and their assistance; especially Annie. At Serenity Shores others got shook up or became frightened when they encountered paranormal activity. Most would shake it off and continue with their business, but not Annie. She did not want to ever be in the funeral home alone, especially at night. She was terrified of the dark, even more than I. Though she had a reverence for the dead, she also had a phobia of them.

Annie was aware that several of us worked in the building at night and often alone. She asked how we could stand it and weren't we scared. The men answered that if they came across something spooky, they'd tell it to go away. The women answered that they would mind their business while going about their duties, or that they didn't believe in ghosts and chose to ignore anything that occurred around them.

Due to Annie's fear, the spirits sometimes tried to help her and let her know they weren't going to hurt her and she had nothing to fear. These kind actions backfired, however, and caused her fear to grow.

One way the spirits liked to help Annie was when she wrote obituaries. Our funeral directors often wrote obits as a service to the families. When they were swamped, they handed off this duty to Annie. Most of the time, Annie had never met the families, seen the deceased, or had any information to work from, yet when she composed the obit, it often seemed to write itself. Occasionally, if she left her computer, she would find the obit completely written when she returned.

The families gave rave reviews to each and every obit she wrote. They often said the obits read as if she had known their loved one. At first, this praise made Annie feel pretty good, but then she felt that ghosts were working their magic through her and she didn't like that one bit. After one of these rewrites, she ranted and raved, tossed papers and kicked walls, then stormed out of the building vowing never to return. After calming down, she returned the next day yet swore she'd never write another obit.

Poor Annie's hours were cut severely without the work of the obits and that forced her to take on other responsibilities. In addition to driving all over town to procure doctors' signatures on death certificates, then returning to the funeral home to process them, she also did light housekeeping and shopped for supplies. Because she still needed more hours to fill the void, she began to assist with evening visitations and services.

I was Annie's trainer for a week before she attended to her own families, separate from mine, in a chapel or parlor on her own with me in the next room. I was to teach her proper protocol, how to dress appropriately, and her full duties, as well as show her where everything was located. She followed me like a puppy dog and absorbed everything I taught. But every time she walked past a casket she froze in terror. I asked her why she wanted to work in a funeral home with her fear of the dead. She said that at first she thought it would be neat, but then realized working in a funeral home might help her to overcome her phobia and be the perfect place to face her fear.

I tutored Annie for several days before she felt confident enough to brave being in the funeral home at night with me and begin her week of formal training. Prior to the family arriving on her first evening, I showed her how to run the sound systems, audio equipment, and electronic video equipment for the memorial presentations. She remembered her duties, dressed as she should, and was ready to face the public. She did great until she had to get extra bathroom products from the cooler room.

She returned to the chapel with her arms full of toweling and toilet paper but shook like a leaf. She said the cooler room door kept trying to close while she was in the room, the lights flickered, and the area around the door got frosty cold while she was in there. She let me know, strongly, that she would never go into that room again. I made a mental note to ask the Doorman to keep still if she was working at night.

Throughout the evening Annie did her job well, but with an air of tense anxiety. She jumped every time someone walked up to her to ask a question. In her jumpy state, I gently refreshed her memory on the cleaning that she was required to do after everyone left for the night. She nodded her head, had the bags for trash stashed nearby, and seemed to be ready and willing. I breathed a sigh of relief thinking that the end of the night would go off without a hitch; at least, I did until the last visitor prepared to leave the mortuary.

I turned to let her know it was okay to begin the night's cleanup, and found she was nowhere to be seen. I locked up all over the building, and looked for and called out to her as I went from room to room. I had a good idea that she had taken off, but honestly wasn't sure. I looked in every room, including the prep room and dressing room that had electronic locks that only certain people knew the codes for. I found no Annie. I got smart and looked in the parking lot. She and her car were gone. I finished up on my own, locked up, and went home.

I wondered if she would show up for work the next evening. She did. We were having a quiet and simple service that evening, so the night wouldn't be a long one. Things ended quickly, and I was able to get her to stay after everyone left. She apologized for taking off so secretively the previous evening.

As the week wore on, however, Annie didn't become any more relaxed. I had already discussed Annie with the Doorman spirit, and he had signaled that he would cooperate when she was around. That didn't make any difference, as apparently Annie could feel his energy. She now refused to exit the building down the employee hallway, especially on one evening in particular.

That evening, she stated that she felt a horribly cold, icy chill in the middle of the employee hall. She informed me that under no circumstances would she approach the cooler room or even walk past that door. She was close to hysteria and felt that whatever was there didn't want her to go past. To calm her nerves and put her mind at ease, as well as my own, I checked out the hallway. As I entered the area, I felt it, too.

I had felt a lot of spirit chill, but not like this. My skin, through my business jacket, began to ice up and I could see my breath; something wasn't right. The room's heavy, thick metal door was closed and covered in an icy film. An odd fog gathered from under the door, swirling in gossamer clouds as I moved. As I readied myself to open the door, I prepared for whatever was on the other side. Even with the extreme cold, my hands sweated and my heart pounded. I felt like I was about to go into battle. Annie stood in the hall talking, pleading, and crying the entire time.

I took a deep breath and put my hand on the doorknob. It had ice crystals on it. I put my other hand on the door itself and shoved hard. The inner knob hit the wall. I fumbled for the light switch. I found it and turned on the lights while I yelled at what I thought would be some sort of otherworldly entity that had taken possession of the room. No way was this type of spirit shenanigans happening on my watch.

Then, I saw it, the reason for the cold. Beyond the shelves of office and cleaning supplies, I saw that someone had propped open the door to the body cooler.

I didn't know whether to laugh or cry. I looked down at my hands and they were shaking. Even though my jacket was ice cold, I was sweating like it was August. I walked all the way into the room, where I saw that the body cooler had been set to zero degrees Fahrenheit. I thanked all that's holy that no bodies were in the cooler at the time. Knowing that the cooler was empty and needed cleaning, I looked at the cooler's logbook and saw that one of the funeral directors had set the unit so that he could give it a good scrub the next day. It appeared that he had read the zero temperature on the dial to be an "O" for off. It was a natural and honest mistake with a logical, non-ghostly cause.

Annie frantically called my name from her position near the hall entrance. I started to laugh and let her know I was okay and everything was fine. I walked out to assure her that she could pass by safely, but I found her as white as a sheet, shaking like a leaf, and babbling incoherently. I calmed her and let her know what had caused the cold and fog, but she would have nothing to do with the area. Even though she believed me and was getting control of herself, she was too shaken and just wanted out of there.

I escorted her out to her car through one of the back chapel's doors. She got in her vehicle and peeled out of the lot. I didn't blame her one bit for being so frightened and wanting out of there by that time, too.

When I came back in, I did my normal duties, and started laughing at myself for becoming so frightened by something that had a logical explanation. I began to think of how I had gotten wrapped up in Annie's fear, right along with her. Then I began to think of things from her viewpoint.

I realized that just because I'm used to dealing with and living with spirits, that doesn't mean that everyone is. Where I find it a nice and kind thing for a spirit to bring in the paper or move coffee urns, others find it more frightening than finding themselves in the headlights of an oncoming car. I also learned that even I am susceptible to the fear of others. Had I not been unintentionally set into an anxious mode by Annie's fears, I probably would have approached the hallway's cold and fog differently. As I sat alone in the mortuary's kitchen, enjoying one last cup of coffee and waiting for the old cooler to cycle itself down so I could completely turn it off, I laughed in spite of myself.

I knew I owed Annie an apology for not taking her fears more seriously. The next evening, I did exactly that. She appreciated it, too.

Years later, Annie still works in the same funeral home, but she has become hard and irascible in her demeanor. She's grumpy all of the time and acts as if she doesn't like working there. She is her kind, sweet self away from the place. I'm saddened that she's chosen to deal with her fear with anger. She helped me so much; I hope that I can return the favor someday.

CHAPTER 6

THE JOKERS

In every funeral home I've worked in, I've come upon things I cannot explain. Little things happen that drive us employees nuts. And these unexplained things happen not only in the places we work, but also in our homes.

From time to time, we all lose keys, cell phones, and remote controls; we misplace checkbooks, debit cards, and our handheld house phones. We usually find these items and put them back into use. That's because we must have them, we recognize them, we know what they're for, and we're connected to them. We're familiar with the item and it has a purpose in our lives; we have to have it. But to someone unfamiliar with the item, it can appear as a novelty that raises curiosity and leads to questions about what it's for and how it's used.

Many times, that's what spirits do. They pick up a thing out of curiosity, check it out for a while, and then misplace it for us. As they aren't confined to physical restraints, they aren't forced to move like we do. When spirits pick up something to look at it, they and the item can go elsewhere and anywhere.

At Serenity Shores, we found things on the roof that we had lost inside the building. An air conditioning repairman had been on the roof doing some repairs when he located a bag of items up there. He kindly brought the bag into our manager's office. In the bag were car keys to personal vehicles, hearses, and flower vans; garage door openers belonging to employees; and one cell phone that belonged to the funeral home. There were also personal items belonging to various deceased individuals or their family, including photos of loved ones, memorial folders, prayer cards, and extra clothing. By the condition of the items and the dates on the folders and cards, some things had been up there for quite some time while others hadn't been up there even a month.

There seems to be a spirit at the funeral home that likes to grab things and pop them onto the roof after it's done with them. Perhaps the spirit can't remember where he or she pinched it from and puts it all on the roof for safe keeping. We were never quite able to figure that one out. We discerned that it was not one of the employees playing tricks and that if things were missing, especially a few at a time, we should look on the roof.

We often found a number of things up there; many we didn't even know were missing, such as a ring belonging to one of the directors. She had forgotten that she'd lost it; when she thought about it, she hoped she hadn't accidentally buried it with someone. She was glad to find that a spirit had simply moved it onto the roof.

Missing items are one thing; moving things is quite another. On several occasions, I walked into the mortuary to find that the cremation urns had been moved. The first time this happened, it was my boss who found them moved. As I was the last person in the mortuary the evening before and he was the first person to arrive the next day, he wanted to know why I had repositioned the urns. I informed him that I hadn't done so, but he still insisted I put them back where they belonged.

As I entered the beautiful, white-paneled room with luxurious, plush, green carpet where the urns and caskets were displayed, I immediately became aware of the quiet, which was almost deafening. I took a good, long, hard look at the urns; they seemed as if they were positioned where they belonged. Nothing looked out of place. My boss walked in, looked at the urns, and asked how I had repositioned them so quickly. I informed him that I had walked into the room just a few minutes before he did. His suggestion was that I knew what urns had been moved so I knew which ones to reposition. Since I hadn't been working at Serenity Shores long, I did not question his thoughts or argue the issue. I hoped this was some sort of initiation joke. After all, my new co-workers did seem to have great senses of humor.

The next time the urns were moved, they were all off in positioning by one. All thirty urns had been moved one space over to the left. This was done all the way around the room and even to the urns that should have been located over their matching caskets. This was unnerving and had me scratching my head trying to figure out how this was being done and by whom. But I read each tag, dusted the urns as I placed them back on their proper shelves, and the problem was easily fixed. The next time the urns were moved, things were not so easy to fix.

We had just changed our line of urns and increased the items on hand from thirty to forty styles with an extra one of each in stock. We had gotten a large shipment of urns the day before, and I had spent the afternoon placing the overflow in the inventory closet of the display room. We came in the next morning to find the entire urn inventory in the middle of the floor with their storage boxes scattered everywhere and the locked closet door standing wide open. Many of the seasoned funeral directors had no idea which urn may have gone where or even what company produced them. I put in a few hours tidying the urn displays, along with the extra stock. Thank goodness none of the urns were damaged.

I wasn't happy with arranging and putting away the urns again and began to wonder if a spirit could be the cause. I decided to have a talk with any spirits that may have been listening and any other entities that may have been hanging around, too. I also had a slight suspicion that my boss and co-workers felt I was the culprit and that didn't make me feel very good. Since I was going out of town for the weekend, I informed the feisty spirit that he should do his little game while I was gone, to prove me innocent, or he should just stop the antics altogether. The spirit had a choice. I felt silly talking out loud about this, but I had no other explanation for the joke and felt I needed to try something. Apparently, I was heard.

When I next reported in to work, the boss took me into the directors' office immediately. My boss and the other directors apologized profusely for their accusations. They informed me that the urns had been moved again during my absence.

The urns had been relocated to many locations throughout the funeral home. Urns were found on the roof; and since they all knew I am afraid of heights, this was a dead giveaway that I had nothing to do with these antics. They were also found in hearses, in a potted tree, under desks, in sinks, in the refrigerator, by the printer, under pews, and on the embalming table covered with a sheet; which I thought was a nice touch. Urns were found behind computer screens, inside unoccupied caskets along with one occupied casket, behind televisions, in the music library, and next to table and chair legs. The playful spirits sent the entire funeral home staff on an Easter egg hunt for urns. Ten thousand dollars' worth of urns had been treated like toys.

If spirits are in the building, eventually urns are going to get moved around. I have been fortunate to work in five different mortuaries and I've filled in doing various tasks at several others. In every location, I've been told of moving, repositioned, or relocated urns. They just weren't moved as often, or as artistically, as they were at Serenity Shores.

Now caskets are a totally different toy altogether for spirits. Even though movement of caskets doesn't happen often, empty caskets have been found lying in the mortuary kitchen and arrangement rooms on the meeting table, balancing on the couch, positioned near a front door, and standing on their ends leaning up against each other like books on a shelf. We have found microwave ovens in empty caskets, along with plants, clothing, and food from the refrigerator. We've even found parts of caskets in caskets.

Caskets have also opened or closed when they haven't needed to. One afternoon, I was speaking to my supervisor at Sherwood Mortuary and Cremation Service in the hall just outside the casket room. We heard a noise that sounded exactly like a casket lid falling shut, similar to that of a car door closing, but with more finality. When we investigated the sound, we found all the caskets in the room open and the hinges locked in the upright position. We turned to leave the room when we heard the noise again. We turned back around and saw all the casket lids now closed. We gave each other a look with raised eyebrows and walked up to the caskets. Upon inspection, we found that the lids were not only down, but also locked.

We were absolutely amazed. We didn't know what to say to each other. I started humming the theme to *The Twilight Zone* and got a pop in the shoulder from my supervisor as he said, "Don't, you'll piss 'em off." We left the casket room to retrieve a pair of casket keys so that we could unlock and open the twenty-four closed caskets. We were out of the room less than two minutes. Upon our return, we found all the caskets open with the hinges locked in the upright position, and the throws lying on the portion of the lid that covers the feet, just as they should be. My supervisor told me to keep this little incident to myself since some employees would immediately walk out the door if they knew this was happening again.

Of course, there is always the occasional occupied casket found open when it should be closed, and found closed when it should have been left open. This happens rarely and is more often attributed to simple human error or a faulty upright locking hinge.

The furniture in funeral homes isn't immune to ghostly pranks either. On several occasions, we would arrive first thing in the morning to find all the lobby furniture in a stack at one end of the hallway, in a chapel, or even blocking the front doors. The couches, end tables, coffee tables, floor lamps, silk plants, and even the magazines from the coffee tables would be found in a nice stack. That was always a fun and invigorating way to start one's day. Everyone can use a little weight-lifting first thing in the morning; or maybe the spirits just felt the carpet needed a thorough vacuuming.

So the next time you're in bed watching a fabulous movie, think about this. You put the movie on pause and leave your remote control on the bed. You get up because you crave a bottle of water or a candy bar. You get that bottle of water or candy bar from the kitchen and return to your nice, warm, comfy bed. You go to grab the remote but you can't find it, yet you know you left it there on the bed. You find yourself wasting ten minutes looking for the thing. You get frustrated because you really want to watch the rest of that film and you can't do anything to the TV without the remote; you're stuck.

The sudden urge takes hold of you to go to the refrigerator. You feel the need to get something to go with the water or candy bar you retrieved earlier, maybe some ice cream or a glass of milk. You walk into the kitchen. You open the refrigerator door and there's the remote, sitting quietly, chilling next to the eggs and butter. You laugh at yourself because obviously you must have had the remote in your hand when you went into the kitchen earlier. You must have plopped the remote on the refrigerator shelf.

Then you remember you didn't go into the refrigerator to get your treat. The bottles were on the pantry shelf, the candy was on the counter. You never opened the refrigerator. You find yourself wondering how this could be or who could've done this.

That's all right, it happens to all of us. I know that this has happened to me upon several occasions in my own home. One doesn't have to live or work in a funeral home to be visited by joking spirits; we all get visited. Now, you too may hum the theme to *The Twilight Zone*.

While writing this chapter, I misplaced my cell phone along with a set of my car keys. Don't worry, they'll turn up. I think I'll go look in the fridge.

CHAPTER 7

UP PAST THEIR FINAL BEDTIME

I am never bothered by children. I'm like most people in that I feel they're our future. They are to be cared for, nurtured, respected, and most of all, loved. Children see the world as we adults would like to see it, with the hopes and dreams that are lost somewhere along the way. If we are fortunate enough to be around young ones, then maybe we'll also observe and listen to them; even take the time to view the world through their eyes—just long enough to recharge ourselves so we can get back to the real world, in all of its stark harshness, with fairness, grace, strength, and, patience.

Unfortunately, stark harshness is a reality far too often. First responders arriving on the scene of a human tragedy often find the lifeless form of someone who has gone too soon. The police officers, firefighters, paramedics, medical examiners, and detectives work to determine the cause of a young life taken suddenly away. Once their investigation is complete on the child's corpse, we funeral personnel take their bodies into our protective custody, where it now changes from *a corpse* to *the deceased*.

Any mortician will tell you that taking care of a deceased child is the hardest thing we do. When a child dies at someone else's hands, we work tirelessly to put their bodies back together. We clean, embalm, cosmetize, and dress them. We work to make them look natural, as if they were just sleeping. We gingerly and lovingly, often with tears in our eyes and hearts, place the body into the casket for viewing.

While I worked at my first attendant position at Serenity Shores, I loved seeing and hearing the children who attended the funerals with their families, playing and laughing and usually well behaved. Early on, more than one well-seasoned funeral director told me to listen for the sound of kids I couldn't see.

"You mean ghosts?" I asked. The reply was always, "Yep!"

"Okay," I thought to myself, "that's no problem. I've dealt with worse." I was open to seeing these spirits, but I doubted I would see any because the spirit of a child wouldn't want to hang around a mortuary, right? I was wrong.

Most of the incidents I experienced with spirits of children were positive. At times, they were heartwarming or downright funny. At Serenity Shores, there is an incredibly long central corridor that connects two different chapels, leads to four parlors, and then ends at the main lobby with its two large glass doors. At night, with just a few hallway lights and a table lamp on in the lobby, anyone can see a clear reflection of themselves in those doors as they approach them while walking down that long corridor. I walked towards those glass doors quite often, many times knowing that I wasn't alone. On many occasions, I noticed little feet and legs following behind me reflected in the glass doors. I would turn around, thinking that a child had followed me out of a visitation. No one was ever there.

I can't say that I ever really became fully comfortable in these situations, but I tried to have a little fun at a somewhat unnerving time. I was always ready to turn around and say "hi!" to a child. I never saw anyone there, but not wanting to seem rude, I would say "hi!" anyway; it helped to deal with any unease I felt.

The first little one who followed me down that corridor was a girl of about eight years wearing a green tank top, Capri-length white pants with a green vine pattern, and leather sandals. She had shoulder-length, dark blonde hair parted in the middle. I saw her reflection clearly, about two feet behind me, as I walked in the direction of the glass doors. She kicked her feet out to the side and waddled with her arms out like little wings as she imitated my funny, crooked walk. She giggled as she played which put a smile on my face making me wanting to play, too. I'd stop abruptly and turn around, but there was never anyone there.

This same scenario played out on a number of occasions. Some nights one or two little boys, wearing suits and ties, followed me and waddled behind; sometimes little girls in fancy dresses and patent leather shoes giggled and walked funny as the fabric of their crinolines crunched and bounced. Often, my little girl in the green tank top would lead the pack. At times, I felt like the Pied Piper of Hamlin all the while knowing that these beautiful children had all gone through our funeral home. Even though it always unnerved me, I took to calling them *my kids,* and lost all fear of them. That first little girl in the green tank top will always be *my little girl.*

But I knew that they weren't mine. They were here for a short time and were more than likely confused or lost. I had read up on the writings and wisdom of James Van Praagh and knew that, if able, I should help them go home into the light and the loving arms of their parents. So, in my own way, I let them know they had passed and it was safe to move on.

Things would calm down in the hallway after one of my sessions with them and would stay quiet for a number of months; too quiet and very lonely. The spirit children unnerved me, but they also made me feel good. During their play, the energy in that corridor made me feel like I too was a child again with the innocence of youth. The spirit children that crossed over from the long corridor are mostly now at peace. They went home easily, but not all do.

One afternoon, I arrived at work to set up the parlors and chapels because we had several visitations that evening located throughout the building. I was put in charge of the visitation for a five-year-old girl who had been murdered, and I knew this was going to be a bad night. The energy in the entire building was desperate and heavy. The atmosphere in the chapel was cold and hopeless with people losing control. Fights broke out, couples argued, many people were distraught.

The other visitations and services went well and ended early. The heaviness of the hearts in my chapel had worked its way into the rest of the building, causing others to feel uncomfortable and leave before their scheduled time. My spry, elderly friend and co-worker, Agnes, finished with her family in the other chapel and slowly entered my chapel's lobby. She said she would stay and help me clean up. She wanted to do some little part for this child in any way she could.

When everyone had finally left the little girl's visitation, we two tired, quiet, and greatly saddened women did a quick job cleaning the entrance, bathrooms, and chapel. As we picked up the last of the many tissues, we heard a child crying. We looked at each other, acknowledging that we'd both heard it and weren't crazy. Thank goodness we were done, because all we wanted to do was lock up and get out of there.

We had to approach the casket containing the little girl to pick up flower petals that had fallen on the floor and make our way out of the chapel. As we got closer to the casket, with plastic trash bags in hand, the crying grew louder and clearer. The crying had originally sounded far away, as if in another world, but now it was somewhere in the room with us, and we seemed to be moving closer to it.

We wondered if, perhaps, someone had put a sound box in the casket as a joke. We gulped, looked around the inside and outside of the casket, as well as underneath and behind it, and found nothing.

The crying changed; it now moved all around us. The crying had acquired a life of its own. We looked at each other, grabbed onto each other's hand, and moved quickly out of the building, locking up and turning off lights as we went.

When we had set the alarm and gone out the employee door, we arrived at our cars and realized we still had the trash bags in our hands. We didn't know whether to laugh, cry, or scream. We leaned against our cars and burst out laughing. Agnes hadn't moved that fast in a long time and was a little winded so I took the trash bag out of her hand and flung both of them into the dumpster. We were okay now, we hoped. Whatever caused the crying sound was away from us and we could head home.

Agnes pulled out of the parking lot immediately. It was such a beautifully crisp winter night with stars so twinkly bright that I decided to take a moment to open the visor on my car's moon-roof and let in some night. I desperately needed some beauty and serenity.

I moved back the visor exposing the glass of the moon-roof window and saw something that I'd only heard about in spooky movies. Drawn in the frost on the moon-roof window was a very unhappy face with the words *I'm cold* printed next to it in a child's scrawl.

I gasped, took a quick glance toward the building, turned back to the moon-roof, and wiped the marked moisture off the glass. It came right back. I dug a rag out of my glove compartment and rubbed on the glass until it squeaked. Breathing a sigh of relief, I looked closely at the glass; the images slowly returned. I started to shake with fright and felt as if there was no air to breathe.

I roughly closed the moon-roof visor and hurriedly opened the car door to let in the fresh night air. Each breath got easier and easier to draw in. All I had to figure out now was how to stop shaking so I could drive. I was tempted to see if the graffiti was still there, but didn't dare. After a few minutes, I closed the car door, rolled down the windows, turned on my car stereo, and drove home.

Thankfully, my husband was home when I got there. I let him know about the evening's stress, along with the marks on the moon-roof window. He immediately went out to the garage and tried to clean it off with window cleaner. When he came back inside, he was chilled to the bone.

"Did you drive home with the air conditioning on? It's freezing in that thing," he remarked. "I couldn't clean it off, either. Me thinks you got yourself a visitor." I knew I had a visitor.

I showed this odd manifestation to several people who tried to clean it off, to no avail. A week later, I had the car detailed at a local carwash; they noticed the graffiti and made a valiant effort to remove it. I told them not to waste their time but they wouldn't listen. The men cleaning the windows had a great reverence for ghostly phenomena. When the graffiti kept reappearing, several of them blessed themselves with the sign of the cross.

In addition to the car washers and family members who worked on the moon-roof graffiti, a psychic healer, who can often clear manifestations, took her turn at clearing my car. She was unsuccessful as well. At that point, I decided to learn to live with the marks and accept the fact that my car was occasionally cold inside, whether it was the middle of summer or the dead of winter with the heater running. The spirit of the little girl had decided to take up residence in my car.

That spirit graffiti stayed on the moon-roof for more than a year, along with the occasional chilling. Then, just as suddenly as it appeared, it disappeared. I found out through a relative of mine who watches every bit of news that she can that the person who had killed the little girl had finally been caught. I never figured out why the child felt the need to mark my car or stay with me. I do know that she did not want to be forgotten. I believe that she is at peace now. She had something that had to get taken care of before she could move on. She must have felt that her little spirit would be safe with me; which it was.

The horrible individual who sent the little girl across far too soon has been found guilty and is paying the price for this heinous crime.

A close and reliable associate, who is still employed at Serenity Shores and also very sensitive to spirits, has told me that the child spirits are once again active and have definitely returned. She tells me about children playing in the corridor and following her, along with my little girl with the green tank top.

These child spirits don't bother her. She's only bothered by the sound of a child crying; it sometimes follows her around the building. I am teaching my friend how to work with this spirit. It is yet another child who has crossed over due to the hands of another. This tragedy never seems to end.

Little Kyle was all of eight years old. He was in a body bag in the cooler of Sherwood Mortuary and Cremation Service. What had happened to Kyle, no one knew, but his body was released into my custody from a hospital. I felt that he should have gone to the Medical Examiner's Office, but the hospital staff disagreed.

When I brought little Kyle into the funeral home, I tried to contact his parents to set up an appointment with them; they couldn't be reached. To a point, this is understandable due to bereavement, but he lay in our cooler for three days before any of my calls were returned.

Several days after that, his parents finally arrived at the funeral home. They couldn't make up their minds about what kind of service to have or the final disposition of the body, and they demanded his death certificate immediately. The state didn't issue death certificates without a final disposition decided upon, so the parents took home the information and pricing that they needed for various services and left the funeral home in a huff. Even with all the information in their hands, I somehow knew this wasn't going to go down easily.

From the first day I'd taken Kyle's body into custody, I had nightmares on a regular basis; dreams of underfed or tortured children, dreams about money, dreams where money was harming children. I had odd dreams about copper mines and turquoise jewelry. Night after night the dreams came and grew in intensity.

After Kyle's parents came into the funeral home, he began appearing in the nightmares, too. He would run up to me and put odd-looking things in his mouth. Sometimes he would be crying in a bathroom, curled up under the sink, naked and cold, putting something in his mouth that he'd picked up off the floor. I tried to reach out and stop him, but couldn't. I wanted to get into that bathroom, cover him with a blanket, and spirit him away after getting him to spit out whatever was in his mouth, but I couldn't. I awoke many nights drenched in sweat, crying, and holding onto my knees while asking, "What happened to you, little guy?"

Several days later, the parents returned. They'd made the decision for burial and wanted to have him embalmed. They paid the bill in cash, set the date, picked out the casket, and handed me his clothes while asking how quickly they could have the death certificate. All seemed to be moving along nicely now, until later that night.

Instead of going home that evening, I decided to help out a co-worker who wasn't feeling well. I sent her home early and finished up her service. Before the family left for the evening, one of their children, a ten-year-old boy, motioned for me to come closer to him. When I did, he grabbed onto the collar of my jacket and pulled me in close.

"You've got to help Kyle. It's not right. Okay?" he whispered into my ear. He let loose of my collar, but I was awestruck and silent while staring into his eyes.

"Okay?" he firmly asked again.

"Um, okay," was all I could say. He smiled, let out a sigh of relief, and left with his family.

That night when I finally got to sleep, I had another dream. Kyle was in the dream and very persistent. I could clearly hear him pleading, "Help me!" while he wore only a diaper and sat on a mountain of shiny, copper pennies. "Help me! Help me!" The pleas reached a crescendo that caused me to violently wake up.

I shook off the fog of sleep and realized that I could still hear "Help me!" in a child's voice somewhere in my house. I hadn't been dreaming the words, and I wasn't the only one who could hear him. My dogs were looking about the room, but not barking.

I cautiously searched my house for the voice, which seemed to be coming from everywhere and nowhere. I heard coins hitting the floor, coins being handled, coins dropping into a piggy bank. I heard water running and toilets flushing, yet there was no evidence of either happening. I began to smell the warmth of copper pipes when they're heated. I looked everywhere making sure that nothing was wrong with my house and knew an answer had to be found as I had to embalm the boy in the morning.

As I wandered about the house trying to figure out what to do, the child's voice began to say something different. I knew that Kyle's spirit was trying to tell me something. I asked him to repeat it; it came back almost in a yell, "Not my mommy!" I heard it clearly that time, but he repeated it several times anyway.

I had to get some kind of answer to this and needed to think clearly, so I splashed cold water onto my face and noticed my teeth in the mirror. They had the appearance of being blue, as if I'd just eaten a blue snow cone. With no logical explanation, seeing my teeth this way startled me. I began to wonder if this had something to do with Kyle.

I began to hear coins dropping again, behind me on the bathroom floor. When I turned around, the sound moved onto the bathroom counter. When I turned back to the counter, there, on top of my toothbrush, was a mound of pennies. Even though this was unnerving and freaky, I stayed calm. Obviously, there was some connection between the color of my teeth, teeth themselves, and coins. I needed to do some research on the computer.

I found information on people who have a bad habit of sucking on coins and the discoloration to their teeth that results. I thought I knew what to do. The child's voice had slowed and sounded tired.

"Kyle," I said to the voice, "if that's you, rest easy now, little one. I think I've got it." I heard a child's weakening cry that faded into nothing.

The next morning, I arrived early at the funeral home and went into the cooler to pull Kyle's body out to acclimate it prior to embalming. I prepared myself to examine his teeth; if they were discolored, I'd make a call. If not, I'd imagined it all and shouldn't drink tea so late at night.

I gently lifted this beautiful child off the cooler shelf. He was much too light for a normal eight-year-old. As I carried his lifeless body down the hall and into the prep room, almost every organ in my body began to ache. My stomach churned and my ears rang. My head ached and pounded; I felt as if I were floating. I saw events unfold through his eyes. I saw his parents leaning over him, yelling at him, forcing him to put something in his mouth. I began to taste something hard, metallic, and copper.

I made my way into the prep room and laid his little body onto the embalming table. After donning a pair of gloves, I unzipped the body bag he was in and unwrapped the clean, white sheet that served as a shroud for the child. I positioned his head and looked upon his malnourished, ashen face. I opened his mouth and looked at his teeth. They were the same color as I'd seen on my own teeth.

I called the Medical Examiner's Office and made the report. I was immediately connected with an investigator who told me to stand by the phone and not allow anyone else to touch the body. The investigator called back and informed me they would be there shortly to take his body into their custody.

With the M.E. on his way to pick up Kyle, I knew I would never see him again. I bent down over his little head and gently kissed his cold brow.

"All will get sorted out now," I told him with tears in my eyes. "Don't you worry anymore. Sweet dreams, little man."

Morticians are often the last people to whom the dead can speak. Dead men do tell tales and we often hear what the dead have to say, just as I heard one special little boy who wanted to make things right and bring the truth to light.

Rest in peace now, little Kyle. May flights of angels sing thee to thy rest.

CHAPTER 8

LITTLE ONES KNOW

At every funeral home I've worked in, I have had the privilege of witnessing living children interact with their deceased loved ones. By their mere actions, children are proof positive that we can interact with the dead and life after death does exist.

One afternoon at Serenity Shores, a family said their final good-byes to their deceased grandfather. With the family was a beautiful five-year-old girl dressed as if she was going to a party. Her long, dark hair flowed in ringlets with peach satin ribbons clipped just above her ears. The ribbons perfectly matched her peach taffeta party dress with a matching sash and big, flouncy bow. The entire family had spent some quiet time together at the casket, and then moved into the chapel pews.

I saw the little girl speak politely to her mother and then, with a determined demeanor, walk up the aisle to the casket. I had placed a casket chair to the right side of the deceased. These chairs are upholstered on the seat, back, and arms, similar to a barstool, but specially designed so that the right armrest is lower than the left which allows a person to sit and lean over the casket comfortably without danger of toppling the casket. The little girl climbed onto the casket chair's seat to sit with her grandpa.

She had been sitting with him for quite some time when I approached the casket with a late delivery of flowers. She was attentively looking at her grandpa and holding his cold, wrinkled hands. As I positioned the bouquet, I overheard her say, "Okay, Gampa, I'll be sure to do that for you."

No adults were close by to help the child so I asked her if there was anything she needed; I also wanted to check out the situation and her positioning for her welfare and the funeral home's liability.

"Oh, no, thank you," She politely replied. "I'm just sitting here talking to my gampa. He's listening to me real good and telling me lots of good stuff. Him also told me to tell you thank you for dressing him so nice. And, him does look really nice."

At this point she stopped speaking, turned toward her grandpa, and gave him her full attention. She then turned to me and said, "Oh, I sorry. Gampa told me that I shoulda said *he* looks really nice, not *him* looks really nice."

"Aw, honey, that's okay," I told her. Then, turning my head toward her grandpa, I uttered, "Thank you, sir."

I turned to take my leave and make my way to my post in the chapel's lobby, when I was stopped dead in my tracks by the soft voice of an elderly man saying, "You're most welcome, dear lady."

I slowly turned my head toward the little girl and her grandpa in the casket. No men were in the area, so I questioningly pointed in his direction while looking at the child. She quietly nodded with a little smile on her face as a tear slid down her cheek. I returned her nod with a caring smile as she raised her left hand and waved bye-bye to me. I turned and continued my walk to the lobby.

Children who like to spend time with their deceased relatives also are not the least bit shy about letting others know they can see their loved one's spirit. Many times, while working a service in a chapel or church, I have seen children pointing and shouting out during a sermon, "Loo-kee, Nana's an angel now!" or "Bye-bye, Grandpa" as they innocently wave toward something that they follow with their little heads and eyes.

Children also seem to have no qualms about playing or talking with the spirits of children. After all, to them another kid is just another kid, whether alive or in spirit.

One warm, spring afternoon in the tiniest chapel at Serenity Shores, three young boys ranging in age from four to eight years were in attendance for the visitation and service of a relative. For a while, they sat quietly in the pews, amusing themselves and reading books, but I knew this wouldn't last as children do get bored no matter how well behaved they are.

When the chapel began to fill with people for the service, my attention was directed toward the youngest of the boys, who was crying miserably and looking at a chair in the corner of the lobby occupied by a corpulent woman in her mid-fifties. The distraught child made his way to me and through his sobs, asked me to get his aunt out of the chair because she was sitting on someone who couldn't get out from under her. This made no sense to me as I saw no one under the portly woman. The eldest of the boys approached and stated, "He wants you to get his aunt to move from that chair; she's sitting on his cousin, Jeremy."

"She's what?" I asked incredulously.

Exasperatedly, he answered, "Really, she's sitting on Jeremy; she won't move for us, she never does. Could you get her to move, please?"

I wondered what I should do as this is something that is not covered in mortuary school. I decided to indulge the boy's wishes. The woman looked terribly uncomfortable in the chair anyway, so I devised a plan.

I approached the woman who was now shifting her weight from side to side in the chair.

"Excuse me, but you look uncomfortable in this chair," I told her. "May I offer you *my* chair over here?"

"Oh, thank you," she gratefully replied. "This chair feels as if I'm sitting on something; it's really lumpy, you know. You folks shouldn't have furniture in here like that."

I thanked her for the information and assured her that I would speak to my manager about it. She walked with me over to the chair across the lobby and found it to be just right.

The three boys immediately surrounded the now-empty chair and acted as if they were talking intently with someone; someone just about their size. I was transfixed by the boys' behavior and movements; they moved as if they were helping someone get up out of the chair. They walked into the chapel with a gap between them just about the size of another child and politely entered the pews while chatting away with the blank space between them.

During the service, the three continued to sit together in the same pew with a space between the first two boys. After the service, the boys went into the parking lot to play. When I poked my head out to check on them, there were four boys playing together in the lot. I knew that three had exited the building, shook my head to be certain of not seeing things, and took a recount: one, two, three, four boys.

People began to leave the service, and a woman called the boys into the chapel. I watched out the window as the four boys walked toward the door. The boys walked into the lobby in the same spacing that they were in while approaching the door, but only three entered. I poked my head out the door looking for the fourth; he was nowhere to be found.

Shortly afterward, the woman who had called them in earlier walked up to me with a kind smile on her face and offered me her hand.

"I wanted to thank you for helping my nephew," she said. "He gets in situations like that a lot. I guess Bobby was pretty upset."

I didn't know what to say, but let her know it was all right, to which she said, "Bobby used to always stick up for my Jeremy when he was alive, too. You'd have thought that they were brothers instead of cousins. I just wish my sister would quit sitting on him. Thanks again for listening to Bobby and the boys." She gave me a little hug, gathered up her things, and left.

It took a moment for what she'd said to sink in. When it did, all I could think of was, "Poor Jeremy!"

The first time it was brought to my attention that children are able to see, hear, and interact with the spirits of other children was in the tiniest chapel in Serenity Shores. A family had come to pay their last respects to the beloved patriarch of their family.

The youngest member of the group was a little girl about the age of four with long, blond hair. She was dressed in her favorite party dress with white, lace-trimmed socks and shiny, black patent-leather shoes.

As is normal with children, she got bored after awhile and began to roam the open hallway just off the chapel. I heard her there, near the restrooms, speaking to other children. I knew she was the only child in the building and thought her voice was echoing off the walls.

While I stood watch in the small lobby, she walked past me and abruptly turned back toward me with a very confident air and her little hands on her hips. She looked around the lobby as if assessing the building and proudly informed me in the endearing speech that only a four-year-old can do, "I likes this place!"

"You do?" I smiled.

"Yep, there's a lot of kids to play with here," she replied.

"There are? Where?" I asked.

She pointed behind me to the adjoining hall's doorway and impatiently responded, "Right there, in the hall."

I turned my head toward the area and neither saw nor heard anything.

"They're right there, looking around the door at you. Why don't you wave to them? They're waving at you. Don't be rude!" I turned my head and waved toward the seemingly empty doorway.

"They say that they know you and try to play with you, but you don't play back. Why you do that?"

"I'm sorry," I told this intelligent and articulate child, "but sometimes, when we get older, we can't see things as well as we used to when we were young."

"Well, that's just silly. If I can see them, you can, too. That's just silly!" She then turned, walked haughtily into the chapel, and was done with her audience with me.

A short time later, the girls' mother approached me in the hallway.

"My little girl thinks you're *silly* because you can't see the kids in the hall that she *can* see," she said. "I just want to apologize for her expression. I hope you don't think she's a touch off or anything for what she sees."

I reassured her I thought she was fine and that I, too, had had unique experiences similar to her daughter's. I could see the stress of the situation fall off the mother's shoulders; she knew she was in a safe zone.

We had an interesting talk about her little girl; how she knew things were going to happen, and how she knew her grandpa had died before the rest of the family did. Her mother also spoke to me of premonitions that her young daughter had that involved her own young demise; we both hoped that this one never came to pass.

When we finished chatting and she had dried her tears, she said, "You know—I can almost hear the other children she's playing with. Why can't I see them?" I didn't know what to tell her since I could hear them exceptionally well now, but I still couldn't see them either.

When the time came for the family to head home, the precocious little four-year-old medium took me aside one last time. She reminded me not to be rude to the other kids and the people like them in the funeral *house*.

"They likes you," she said kindly, then left the funeral home with her family.

Because she was so articulate and so precocious, I wondered silently to myself why she hadn't said good-bye to me; she had insisted upon being polite and this struck me as odd. As she walked hand in hand with her mommy toward their car, she suddenly stopped, turned toward me standing at the door, and said, "Because I can't say good-bye yet."

Several years passed when, one afternoon while at home in my bedroom playing with my cats, an overwhelming feeling of sadness suddenly engulfed me. Out of nowhere and for no reason I could understand at the time, I began to cry as if someone had just ripped my heart out.

Through my sobs and my cats trying to console me, I became aware of the sound of little feet skipping playfully through my house. My cats could hear this sound as well and looked in the direction it was coming from. I calmed and continued to listen. The melodious sound of a child's laughter accompanied the skipping that moved closer to my room.

The skipping and laughter stopped just outside my bedroom door. My cats now focused intently on the open door, flicking their tails as if they were ready to play with whomever or whatever had just stopped there. I, on the other hand, could see nothing, but then I heard the precocious voice of the little girl say ever so softly, "I likes this place, too. *Now*, I say good-bye."

CHAPTER 9

THEY SIT VIGIL

Just as some people sit for hours next to the bed of a loved one in the hospital, many sit with the body of a loved one who has passed. While sitting vigil is a cultural or religious norm for some, others feel it is a last gift for the deceased, offering respect and protection while giving strength and closure to the living.

Sadly, many people who would like to have someone sit with them have no one left who can do this caring task. They often do not have anyone visit them, even during a regular viewing. That's when they receive visitors who themselves have passed on.

Some spirits who show up to sit are wonderful. Others, on the other hand, can be scary. This was the case with one sitter that always unnerved me no matter how often I saw him. This entity is one of the few dark spirits at Serenity Shores. He only appeared in one particular parlor while the dead lay in state there with no visitors. Never would he show himself if another living person was in the room or if the lights in that parlor were on.

Every once in awhile, children in attendance at a viewing or service in the southern chapel would let me know a man was in the window of the building next door. That building was actually part of Serenity Shores and housed the parlors adjacent to the main corridor and lobby.

The first time this happened, the children informed me that a man was in there that was dark and kind of scary. They said he stared at them through the window of the parlor. One child said the dark man moved the curtain and looked at them through the glass window, while another said the dark man looked *through* the curtain at them.

When I looked out the window, I saw the curtain move too. No one was supposed to be in that parlor, so I had to go and check it out. While I knew that a body was casketed in that room, I did not like the thought of someone in there and messing around.

Going to the parlor area isn't a long walk, but it certainly felt long that evening. The fall weather was lovely with a slight night breeze and a touch of chill to the air. I entered the lobby through the glass door, which was locked from the outside, and a few yards away from the parlor. After unlocking the door and upon entering, I noticed that the lobby was ice cold. Even with the cooler temperature outside, there was no reason for the extreme chill inside this part of the building. I checked the thermostat and found the air conditioning was off, but the temperature gauge read a chilly forty-eight degrees; no wonder it felt cold.

I opened the parlor door and began to shiver heavily as the room was much colder than the lobby; chilled air hit my face like an arctic blast. As I groped for the light switch, I saw the silhouette of a man sitting across the room in front of the window in a low sloped-back, upholstered chair. The parking lot lights showed through the window, back-lighting him. I was somewhat unnerved due to the heavy presence of dark along with the cold.

"I'm sorry, sir," I said as I shivered, "but no one is allowed in here at this time." I said this as I flicked the switches and turned to face him, but when the lights came on, no one was there.

I looked around the room knowing he had no place to hide and saw that nothing was out of order. I thought it must have been a trick of the lighting or something put into my head by the kids. I checked on the deceased. He was set and ready for his final ride in the morning. Casket closed and locked, memorial print package at the ready, and nothing disturbed. The only odd thing was the extremely uncomfortable cold of the room.

I turned off the lights and just happened to look in the direction of the chair again. There he was, the man in silhouette, in the same comfy chair and facing my direction. Aside from being chilled to the bone, I became mentally frozen as well. I looked right at him and he toward me. I could see the outline of his clothing clearly. He wore a long-sleeved jacket with a flat lapel, a collared shirt, and a fedora slightly cocked on the left side of his head. He sat calmly with his elbows on the arms of the chair and his fingers interlaced on his lap. I heard the distinct sound of calm breathing from his direction, but heard my own breath come out in shivers. His breath became deeper and longer with low, growling rumbles. I brought myself out of my frozen trance and threw the lights back on while not taking my eyes off the chair; in the light, he was gone.

I turned off the lights and stepped into the hallway while trying my best not to look in the direction of the chair, knowing full well that he was there.

"I don't know who you are or why you're here," I said before closing the door, "but, I'm telling you, stop looking through the curtains at those kids. You hear me?" As I walked away, laughter came out of the parlor that sounded so ugly, dark, and cruel that my stomach began to turn. I shook off the feelings of nausea that were beginning to grab onto me, locked up the glass entry door, gathered my wits about me, and went back to the chapel.

Upon my return, a man approached me and put his hand on my shoulder.

"You've got some bad mojo in that room, hon," he said softly but firmly in my ear. "It's been looking through the curtains again as you were walking back over here. Let's go over together and turn those lights on and leave them on."

"The people in here will see the casket in there with the lights on. They have enough on their minds right now," I said to him.

"No one at this funeral is going to care," he calmly said. "They're used to seeing caskets lately. We can't let him get a good look at our kids. Trust me. Let's go."

The man, with his calm and confident manner, had me convinced, and together we went back over to the parlor. As I unlocked the glass door once again, my escort became violently ill. He doubled over, couldn't stand, and began sweating profusely. An unknown force kept him from entering the building, which made me very angry. He pleaded with me not to go in as I charged through the door and into the lobby's cold.

"First, you scare my kids, then you turn my dead guy into a Popsicle, now you make a guy puke. You're outta here!" I angrily bellowed as I moved through the lobby and stormed into the parlor. I threw open the door and saw his silhouette sitting there as I entered, but didn't care.

"Okay, buddy," I said while flicking on the light switch, "I'm turning these lights on and you're gonna get the hell outta here. Go back where you came from, you jerk." And I left the room, slamming the door and leaving the lights on.

My escort was still doubled over by the front door. As I touched him, his sick feeling disappeared. He stood up and asked what had happened. I told him I wasn't sure, but all I knew for certain was that I'd gotten mad.

The rest of the evening went off without a hitch. My only dread was going back into the parlor wing to turn those lights off as they had to be off for the alarm to set. My escort again approached me just before his group left and insisted upon accompanying me to the parlor wing to shut off the lights. Since the children had left, turning off the lights now wouldn't be a problem.

The cold was still in the parlor's lobby as we entered. My chivalrous escort told me he had prepared himself this time and would now be able to make his way into the building without getting ill. He stood just outside the door to the parlor as I entered quickly to turn off the lights. When the lights went out, the silhouette reappeared in the chair. This time, the entity moved his hands onto the arms of the chair and slowly stood up. I scurried out of the room and slammed the door. My escort, prepared as he was, began to vomit again. He knelt on the floor, holding his gut. I could tell the thing in the room was approaching as the low growl came closer to the other side of the door. I prayed while I pulled my escort up and told him to move his ass.

When we got out of the door and I locked down that wing, he felt normal again as if nothing had happened.

"You know what?" he breathlessly asked while holding onto his belly, "I don't think I ever want to come to this building again, even if I'm dead." I agreed with him. He informed me that we shouldn't discuss any of this with the family or his buddies whatsoever, as they thought he was a bit on the weird side anyway. I asked how he knew about the entity in the parlor. His reply was that he knew, he *just knew*, and left it at that.

After everyone left, I bolted the chapel doors and proceeded to close up the building for the night. Although I remembered the man's vomit hadn't been cleaned up outside the parlor door, I decided that this night it could wait until morning. I had no intention of going near the parlor.

The next morning, I was scheduled to take to the cemetery the deceased from the parlor containing the silhouette entity. I arrived early but found that my boss had arrived even earlier and had everything loaded for the final ride. After we set up for the service at the cemetery, we had some time to kill before the family arrived. My boss pulled a chair from under the awning, sat it in the early morning sun and sighed.

As he shakily lit a cigarette, he casually asked if I'd turned the air conditioning on in the parlor wing. He found it off when he arrived in the wee hours of the morning, but the area was deathly cold to him. The cold helped him as he cleaned up the puddle of vomit that someone had left outside of the parlor door, and he asked if I knew anything about that, too.

I answered his questions and informed him of what had occurred the night before. As we spoke he became very nervous and pale; I asked if he was okay. He got a faraway look in his eye and said, "So, he *is* back. I thought I felt something in there the past few days," and bowed his head. After taking a deep breath and a long drag on his cigarette, he said he didn't want to discuss it any further and asked that I not speak of the incident, or any future episodes, with the other employees.

On several other occasions I noticed Mr. Silhouette and chose to show him some attitude each and every time. He never became as forceful again and I never knew which bodies would bring his presence. When he did show up, he would always sit vigil in that parlor, in that chair, if a deceased person had no one or few interested parties visit. He was a pain and still gives me a dark feeling anytime I think of him.

My chivalrous escort attended a service that I directed at Sherwood Mortuary and Cremation Service a number of months later.

He approached me and asked, "So, you don't work at Serenity Shores anymore?" When I informed him that I'd moved on, he said, "That's good. Something not so good is going to happen over there. There's a lot of good energy and spirits there, but there's also a few bad ones. Like him and the imp in the hallway near the chairs. Glad you're out of there." That's all that we said; I never saw him again at any other funeral.

At times we find that no one shows up to the visitation, service, or actual burial for a deceased person. No matter the reason, at least we're there. Those of us in charge of the body are present along with those who have been commissioned to preside over the spiritual needs of the deceased.

One evening, during a blustery and wet storm, I was alone at Serenity Shores waiting patiently for the many visitors that I had been told would be arriving. For nearly an hour I sat alone in the south chapel with the deceased and began to doubt that anyone would show up with a storm raging.

When I stepped into the music room to take a sip of warm coffee, the wind blew violently—just like in an old spooky movie—and the main doors of the chapel flew wide open. Thunder and lightning crashed, making the lights go out as the rain poured outside. I abruptly set down my cup and ran to the front doors to close them against the elements.

When the lights came back on and the doors were shut, I heard voices behind me in the chapel. Five dear, sweet, elderly ladies had arrived as if by magic. They wore clear plastic rain bonnets and rain coats of many colors and patterns. They each carried umbrellas along with knitting baskets while one also had a thermos. They were chatting away about the awful weather. I distinctly heard one of them utter, "You know, he just shouldn't have made it like this tonight; he knew we were heading out!"

"Shush, she'll hear you," another one said, "would you shush?"

I approached this sweet group and noticed they were soaked. Rainwater dripped off their clothes and umbrellas and onto the pews and carpet.

"You're absolutely soaked," I said compassionately. "I'll get something to help you dry off."

"No need, dear," replied a silver-haired, stately woman of about seventy or so; I got the impression that she was their spokesperson. "We'll have it taken care of in a jiffy." I felt the need to help these women anyway and didn't want them to catch their death of cold or worse. I ran to the kitchen's linen closet and grabbed a small bucket and some soft towels.

When I returned, they were calmly sitting in the pews they had just dripped water onto. I was concerned that they would catch their death sitting on the wet upholstery, and was also concerned that my boss would not like all the damp seats and carpet. I was chatting with them and checking the area as I sat down the bucket and towels.

"No need dear," the stately woman said again. "As I said, we took care of it, spit-spot. But, thank you anyway."

As I looked around, I noticed that the raincoats, galoshes, bonnets, hats, and all five umbrellas were laid neatly on a chair reserved for clergy near the dais; they were as dry as if they'd been sitting there for hours. Not a puddle or drop of water could be found anywhere. I looked closer at the women as they chatted together. Some knitted while others enjoyed a cookie that I bet was homemade.

"Would you like some hot chocolate, dear?" the stately woman asked me as she opened the thermos.

"Oh, no, but thank you," I politely replied. "Maybe later? I've got to put these things back." I indicated the bucket and towels.

"Certainly, dear," she answered. "And don't worry, there's plenty more where this came from." I wondered what she'd meant by that as it looked like they only had the one thermos for the five of them.

Unfortunately, no one else showed up at the visitation. I had nothing else to do except be there if the five ladies needed something. I never sat in the chapel with them, but did observe them from my vantage point in the lobby. I saw them go up to the deceased and chat with her. It looked as if they would speak to her and then pause as if she were speaking back. They would nod their heads while seeming to answer her, often looking toward the heavens while holding her hand.

Several times they filled the thermos with water from the lobby water cooler. I approached them and asked if they'd like a pot of hot coffee instead of just water.

"Oh, no thank you, dear," said the stately spokeswoman. "We have oodles and oodles of hot chocolate. Would you like some now?" I politely replied that I didn't think it would be wise for me as hot chocolate *always* gave me heartburn.

One of the ladies, a thin woman of average height with bird-like features, walked up behind me and bent around my left shoulder.

"I guarantee, dear, that our hot chocolate won't give you heartburn," she confided. "Go ahead, try some. You'll like it!"

"I put cinnamon in it just the way you like it!" the spokeswoman chimed in with the sweetest knowing smile on her face. I almost accepted the little cup of hot chocolate, then thought that I'd better not. The level of heartburn that I got with hot chocolate, at that time in my life, was so bad that I'd often be sent to bed, and I couldn't risk that as I had another hour of work yet to go. I explained this to them. They understood and let the issue drop.

Awhile later, I was bored and decided to chat with the women as it was nearly half past eight and I would be locking down the building at nine.

"Excuse me ladies, I think it's wonderful you came out on a night like this to sit with her. She must have been very special to you. Were you close to her?"

"Oh, my dear, this weather doesn't bother *us* one little bit," said the spokeswoman.

Another woman in a definite north Midwestern accent said, "We know her from bingo, dear."

We chatted together about the weather and their knitting projects for a few more minutes. I left their company to check on the storm that seemed to have let up a bit.

As it neared nine o'clock, the women got up, said their final good-byes to their friend, and put their raingear back on. They had already packed away their cookies, thermos, and knitting. I tried to figure out how they had gotten themselves together so fast without my noticing, when the storm suddenly became violent again.

I started to say something to them from the lobby area of the chapel when the spokeswoman said, "We'll be going in just a minute, dear. Our ride is coming!"

The wind blew fiercely and the chapel doors blew open once more. The lights flickered and went out. Thunder boomed overhead as lightning lit up the rain-drenched driveway and street. Rain shot into the lobby like piercing blades, soaking my hair and clothing as I slipped on the rain-soaked rug and fought against the wind to close the doors. The entire building had gone pitch-black. I had my eyes off the group as I yelled for them to take cover. The wind violently picked up a trash can by the front door. As I grabbed the trash can, I saw that the only car in the lot was mine and knew the women's ride hadn't arrived. I hoped their driver hadn't come to any harm in the storm.

I anchored the trash can into a secure corner near the chapel entrance and ran back inside, throwing my weight against the doors to get them closed at last. The building was dark, and I knew those dear sweet ladies would be scared out of their wits. I was a bit shook up myself.

I entered the chapel, wiping rain off of my jacket and face. Rummaging in the pitch-black music room for a flashlight, I yelled above the noise of the storm that everything would be okay and their car wasn't here yet. Upon locating the flashlight, I shined the light on where they had stood. They were gone.

I thought all of that water and hot chocolate must have taken its toll and they had somehow made their way to the ladies' room in the central corridor. As I made my way to look for them, the lights came back on, and I blinked hard at the sudden blinding light. I looked around the chapel and saw that the women's things were gone as well.

Knowing their ride hadn't shown up, I thought they may have become claustrophobic being in a dark mortuary and went to wait for their ride outside, taking their leave through the side door to the left of the casket. I also wondered how they'd moved so quickly. I zoomed out the side door and saw no one there and no cars pulling out of the parking lot or on the road. There were also no wet tire marks under the awning where they would have had to be standing.

Having already locked all the chapel's doors, I went looking through the funeral home for those five special women. They were nowhere to be found. I went out in the rain one more time to look for them, or their ride, and saw no cars except for mine and no women either.

I went back to the chapel to close the casket. This was, and always will be, one of the most humbling experiences I have as a mortician. Others say this is just part of the job or something to get done so the deceased can be put in the ground. I don't look at it that way. I understand the honor and extreme responsibility of being the last person on earth to view the face of the dead. I always take my time, say a prayer, and wish them a safe journey with a peaceful rest.

As I prepared to close the casket after this strange night, I noticed something in the hands of the deceased that hadn't been there earlier. She now held three items that were plainly visible: one perfect red rose with a note attached that said, "To the Love of My Life. Welcome Home. I've Missed You!"; a note written with bright pink ink in a child's scrawl, "I'm waiting for you in heaven, Grandma"; and a photo of a child in a casket.

I was close to tears. After quietly closing the casket, I asked myself when these items could have been placed in her hand and by whom. They weren't there earlier when I was running about looking for the women. I would have noticed the beautiful red rose.

As I entered the lobby, I noticed something written on the exposed pages of the guest book that the five ladies had neglected to sign. In bright pink ink, in the same child's scrawl as on the note in the casket, was written "Thank you for taking care of my grandma" followed by a little pink heart.

I had no idea what to think of this and couldn't breathe for a second or two. It wasn't written in the book earlier; I would have noticed. I felt the sudden need to just go home, so I locked up, dashed to my car to avoid the downpour, and headed out.

I don't remember the drive home. I just know I arrived safely. My mind was filled with thoughts of the evening; from the ladies' thermos water becoming fragrant hot chocolate, to their dramatically mysterious arrival and departure, and the lack of visitors, along with the final gifts and note of thanks.

Upon my arrival, my husband told me he had found a packet of hot chocolate mix on the shelf. He didn't know it was there but, since the weather was so bad, he had made some for us. At this point, the hot chocolate sounded good. When my heartburn would flare, as I knew it would, my antacids would be close by.

I enjoyed that cup of warm, chocolaty velvet that had just a touch of cinnamon. There was enough in the packet for two cups, and for the first time in many years, I didn't get heartburn. We knew we had to get this brand again.

My husband had tossed out the empty packet so we went through the trash. We couldn't find the package and had no idea where it had come from; my husband said it was sitting on the shelf next to the coffee. He couldn't recall the brand name either, but he remembered a photo on the packet of an old woman sitting in a rocking chair, knitting, with a thermos on the floor next to her. Again, I didn't know what to think, but I had a good idea.

Ever since I drank that unknown elixir, I no longer get heartburn when I drink hot chocolate. I often wonder if it was mere coincidence, a touch of divine intervention, or both.

I don't know if these ladies or the silhouette entity are spirits of those who have lived, foreboding specters, or angels in street clothes. Whatever these frighteningly creepy, wonderfully spooky, and uniquely caring spirits are remains to be seen. But I do know that not everyone sitting at a service is who they appear to be, and there's more in the dark than just the dark. In either case, whichever appears and for whatever reason, at least the dead are not alone.

CHAPTER 10

THEY COME A-KNOCKIN'

Some people feel that a funeral home is *the* place to deposit a dead body, whether it happens to be their own or someone else's. People have been known to commit suicide at a funeral home, while others leave their sick handiwork at our door when they commit murder. We often suspect that they feel they're doing us a favor and saving us a trip, or that we'll be kind enough to dispose of the evidence. When either gruesome event occurs, however, there is a set procedure we follow and the first step is to call the police.

Included in the throngs of trained people who arrive on the scene in our city is the Crisis Management and Counseling team. These compassionate and highly trained individuals come to offer us crisis counseling. Once the team members realize that we're on the same page with them due to the nature of our profession, we often redirect them to on-lookers who may have unknowingly stumbled upon the grisly sight or are transfixed by the organized chaos of the situation.

After the authorities determine that the person is indeed deceased, the medical examiner arrives to formally pronounce the body as being dead and take it into their custody. Our funeral home area now turns into a crime scene or an area of suspicious activity. We're all interviewed by authorities and offered counseling once again.

Whether coldly dumped or looking for their own private peace, these poor, dejected souls have some hostile, angry, confused, and anxious energy with them. These spirits can be the most difficult.

At Blue Willows Mortuary, a quaint and humble facility with a home-like atmosphere, a gentleman had been murdered at the front door several years before I started filling in there. It had been a startling and horrific scene with blood splattered outside on the antique white brick; puddles of pooled blood soaked into the entryway's green indoor-outdoor carpet; and handprints and footprints in blood and mud on the outer walls, front door, and panes of glass. All of us who worked at Blue Willows knew the history of this murder and would sometimes discuss it among ourselves. Some nervously made jokes about the spirit of the murdered man returning to the mortuary to look for his murderer, or seek revenge upon those who wouldn't let him in that night. I didn't dare join in on any of the jokes, as

I had experienced so many paranormal incidents at Serenity Shores by this time.

This type of thing was never covered in the employee handbook or any of the mortuary science textbooks. I often found myself winging it when it came to close encounters with spirits, and I prayed I would never run into the angry spirit of a murdered individual. All that changed one evening during a viewing and vigil for a man of Old World, Eastern European ancestry.

This gentleman's culture specified that the body should never be left unattended. His family had set up a camp-like atmosphere in the huge parking lot in the back of the building. The funeral home had obtained all the necessary fire and camping permits for the family, and I had been brought in to keep the building accessible to them throughout the night. They settled down for the night with a few close family members, mostly women, staying in the funeral home with their loved one. They sat and chatted among themselves on the soft, overstuffed couches in the Victorian-style living room; took quiet strolls in the hallway past the interior doors of the chapel to the right of the living room; headed out the back door for a break or into the chapel to spend some private time with their loved one lying in the casket.

Sitting comfortably in a maroon upholstered wing-back chair placed strategically in the hallway, I could block anyone from mistakenly gaining access to the work rooms of the mortuary. I also could observe the living room and front door area, the chapel and the deceased, as well as the back parking lot.

Several women and one twelve-year-old girl, wearing black lace scarves and hand-embroidered shawls, sat in the living room, chatting and working on some fine embroidery. I was about to get up to stretch my legs when I noticed that one of the middle-aged women began to stare off in the distance, then turned her head toward the front door behind her as if she had heard a noise. She got up and approached the front door where she cautiously put her hand on the doorknob. She contemplatively removed her hand from the knob and put it up to her mouth. She took a deep breath, set her feet, put her hand on the knob again, turned it, and opened the door. She walked out onto the front entry walkway. Seeing this, I rose out of my chair to see what might have given her pause when a loud, blood-curdling scream came from the area. I flew to the front door, along with many others from the parking lot, to find out the cause.

Blood had appeared on the walkway carpeting in puddles that smelled coppery fresh, sickeningly sweet, and warm. I stood on the walk trying to figure out when and how this horrific scene had happened since we had been nearby the entire time and had heard nothing.

Several male members of the family came and took the distraught woman back into the building. I had everyone clear the area, which they did, all except for one tiny woman in her eighties who reminded me of someone in an old black-and-white movie. She stood at the doorjamb gazing upon the pools of blood and signaled for me to come over to her. When I got within arm's length of her she grabbed my jacket sleeve and pulled me aside. With her beautiful European accent she knowingly, yet softly, stated that someone had been murdered there many years earlier, and he was going to come back. He would return that night.

I tried to be logical about it and thought someone had pulled a disgusting, malicious prank. I acknowledged her comment and went to call the police anyway. I was stopped by the young twelve-year-old girl before I could leave the front room and get to the office phone. The girl told me that the blood would be gone in a moment or two and calling the police was not going to have any effect. I stared at the child wondering how she knew what the blood would do and how she knew where I was headed. The elderly woman walked up behind me and asked me to return with her to the doorway. As I watched, the pools of blood decreased and withdrew until they disappeared.

I was astonished and tongue-tied as I stumbled over my words, repeatedly calling the elderly lady *ma'am* as I asked her what had just happened.

"Please to not call me the *ma'am*," the woman said, patting me on the arm. "Please, little one, to call me Mama." She looked intensely into my eyes with caring warmth and the wisdom of the ages.

"It is a good thing we are here with you at this time," she said. "This could have happened when someone else was here and no one could help him. We can help him and keep the danger away from you and the others who work here."

"What danger? What's going on?" I stupidly uttered.

"Just quiet yourself, child," she replied. "The danger is in the death of this poor soul returning; coming back and coming to one of you. This man's death was not an honest death, and he is coming back to seek revenge. This is the last place he drew breath, so this is where he will return and we are thinking it will be tonight. Don't worry, little one. We will care for him."

For some reason, I had complete faith in this little woman and asked if the people who killed him might also return. Mama let me know that those men were going to come to their just end soon enough, but they were not going to come around the funeral home ever again. I wondered what to do now since this is certainly one subject that was never in the employee handbook; I decided to wing it.

Had I not seen the blood and what it had done with my own eyes, I would have thought she was a touch loony. Believing her now, I let Mama know they could do whatever they needed. I asked, though, that they not burn the place down since I could see their bonfire had grown in size from four feet across to nearly ten. Mama said the fire in the back parking lot was now all they needed; they would be careful.

"You did a good thing for my boy lying in there," she said. "We do this thing for you. Just watch and learn, and don't worry. There was a reason you were brought in to be with us this night. We know what we are doing; we've done this before."

I must admit that I unknowingly expected some crystal balls, maybe incense or tarot cards. I was stereotyping, which was ignorant of me. The bonfire glowed brightly with flames shooting high into the air; many of the group had gathered around the open flame, holding hands to form a circle, and chanting quietly.

Mama asked that I lock and bolt the front door, then keep the key with me. Firmly but gently I was told to *just sit* in my chair in the central hallway. This is where she stationed me to observe and learn. Then she let me know that if there came a knocking or pounding on the front door, I was not to answer it. The young girl, who now looked much older than her youthful twelve years, informed me that she would sit nearby; if the knocking or pounding came, she'd let the others know. I was to just stay put.

I locked and bolted the solid oak door. I took a moment to gaze out through the door's little panes. Through the small beveled and etched glass panels, I saw that nothing and no one was out on the front entry walk. As I returned to my chair, I was apprehensive and didn't know if anything was going to happen—I hoped nothing would. I was thinking about what I had seen and smelled on the front patio, when the first knock came.

Then a second knock hit. Then a third. Three raps against the door. Through the glass I saw a man whose clothing and flesh looked to be covered in blood. The man was there yet he wasn't there. He appeared to be solid yet he wasn't. I could see the lights of the front garden and the safety lights of the walkway through his body. He gazed in

one of the little windows as if he was looking for someone and never focused on me or the young girl; both of us
stared wide-eyed at the door. Then as quick as he was there,
he was gone.

The girl cautiously got up.

"I hate this part," she said. "You stay here like Mama
said." I just watched as she exited, past the chapel doors,
and out to the bonfire area.

I could see the girl speaking with Mama and several others when the knocking started again, only louder this time.
The entire humble little building vibrated as the knocking
became pounding; pounding that didn't stop. I heard a male
voice outside the door plaintively calling out "Help me! Let
me in. I know you're in there." Again, I could see the same
face through the glass panel. Again, he was not looking
directly at me but it was as if he knew someone should have
been there. I shifted my gaze to the lowest pane of glass
just above the kick-plate and saw that the spirit's feet were
not touching the ground. The man's image was beginning
to glow an angry red color. I wanted to get up out of that
chair and hide, but I felt as if lack of movement would prevent the specter from seeing me. I was frozen at my post.

The group had completely encircled the fire now. The
chanting was louder and in a language I couldn't understand. As the chanting grew in volume, the pounding got
louder and heavier. The combined sounds were deafening.
I covered my ears with the palms of my hands to muffle
the growing sound. I hoped the windows and door didn't
give way. The ghost pounded and yelled, the group chanted

louder. The sounds were growing and the energy in the building was electric. The room began to smell of fire and blood. Then the lights went out.

I didn't care what Mama told me, I was up and out of that chair and heading toward the group outside. As I ran past the chapel doors in the darkened hall, I was grabbed, gently but firmly, from behind by a man. He was large and muscular; the scent of Aramis cologne flooded over me like a comforting blanket.

"Stay inside, little one," he whispered as he held onto my shoulders. "Let them do what they need to do. He won't get in with me here." He kept his massive hands on my shoulders while gently pulling my back safely into the warmth of his barrel chest as we looked out onto the parking lot and the group by the bonfire. I felt unexpectedly calm even though the pounding at the door continued and the voice had turned to sounds of moaning.

Through the windows in the chapel, we saw the spirit moving, floating a few feet above the ground. The spirit put off a violent red glow brighter than the flames. He ascended into the air above the group around the bonfire. The chanting got louder. I became aware that the pounding had stopped. The spirit appeared to be listening to the chanting and looking toward the group; where earlier he had been writhing in pain, he was now calm and relaxed with relief. His essence, his form, was suspended over the flame of the bonfire. Mama separated herself from the circle and approached the fire while looking directly at the hovering spirit. I could hear her voice; the glow of the flame shone upon her gently moving lips. The spirit looked directly at her and smiled. As he smiled, the aura around him changed from violent red to a glowing white, and finally to the shiny, sparkling blue of night. He then looked to the heavens and was gone.

The flame of the bonfire was immediately extinguished by several male members who had been standing at the ready with buckets of water. All was dark, except for some lights in the parking lot, and all was quiet.

"Now, I must go," my guardian whispered into my ear. "All is done, little one. And I thank you." As he removed his hands from my shoulders, I caught sight of his cuff-links, shirt cuffs, and jacket in the light of the parking lot shining through the chapel windows. When I turned to thank him, he was gone. I stood alone, searching for movement in the dark and wondering where he'd gone off to so quickly, the smell of Aramis still lingering on my jacket.

The lights came back on, and as my eyes adjusted to the light, I looked around for my guardian and saw no one. While standing in the chapel doorway in awe of what had just transpired, Mama walked back into the building. She took a quick look at her son in the casket, gave a small smile in his direction, and went to the ladies' room. I went outside to check on the smoldering pile of embers that had been a roaring blaze just minutes earlier. The men had everything under control and were cleaning up the mess. Upon my return, Mama motioned for me to sit with her on the couch in the living room. The young girl was with her now.

"So, child, I'm thinking that you wish to know what happened here tonight," she said.

"Yes, Mama," was my certain reply.

"The man at the door had been murdered here, viciously, at the front door step, several years ago this very night," she began. "I felt his energy when we came here earlier today to be with my son. We were prepared for his return.

"You see, child, he knew that night he was going to die. He made his way here, to this funeral home, hoping for sanctuary. A friend of his, a man by the name of Tom, worked here at the time and was supposed to be here working that night. Unfortunately for the man, Tom wasn't needed to work after all. But it was fortunate for this Tom, for if he had been here, he'd have been killed, too. I believe the dead man has come back every year, but no one has been here. We took control of his spirit and explained things to him. He accepted the truth and is now at peace with our Heavenly Father above. He won't bother anyone on this earth ever again. He is now truly at peace. Are you all right now, child?" she took hold of my hands and gently patted them.

"Oh, yes, I'll be fine. You had everything under such control. I feel like an idiot for trying to run out into the parking lot. I'm thinking that wouldn't have been such a good idea," I answered.

"No, child, that would not have been a good idea. He may have mistaken you for his friend and lashed out at you. Sometimes they don't see so good when they're on the other side, frightened and angry; remember that. What stopped you?" she replied with an enquiring tilt to her head.

"I was running out to you after the lights went out and someone grabbed me from behind. A big man, not fat, with big, strong, and gentle hands. I think he had on a suit. He let me know I was safe with him and you needed to do what you needed to do. He knew you, so I'm sure he's around here somewhere." At this point, I noticed a tear slide down Mama's cheek.

"Did he smell of cologne and call you 'Little One?'" When I answered yes, she said, "That—was my son."

"Oh, where is he? He disappeared so fast. I'd like to thank him," I said, looking around the area.

"You know where he is, child," she said solemnly and longingly. "I only had the one left." I turned my head in the direction of the casket in the chapel. That's where I'd seen those hands before.

Sometimes people are accidentally killed at or near a funeral home. Such is the case of one gentleman who was hit by a truck while on his motorcycle in front of Mercy Meadows Mortuary and Memory Lawn. The young man passed away just after being air-lifted from the parking lot of the cemetery's main entrance.

Six months after this accident, near the winter holidays, I had the honor to fill in at the cemetery. A man who looked rather dirty and beat up walked into the mortuary building, located on the cemetery grounds. He approached the four of us standing near the front desk and asked where his motorcycle was. When we told him we didn't know anything about his motorcycle, he got a faraway look in his eyes, said okay, and walked back out the door. We looked at each other quizzically. One of the directors poked his head out the door to see which way the man had gone. The lost and forlorn-looking man was nowhere to be found.

Every six months or so, he walks back in and asks the same question. As I write this, it's coming up on Thanksgiving. I'm sure he'll be walking in there again fairly soon.

Then there are those unfortunate souls that choose to end their lives by their own hands at a funeral home. If their spirits make a return visit, they can often reflect their feelings at the time of their suicide, which can leave the living who encounter these spirits knowing what real fear is.

Many years before I started working at Serenity Shores, a man had taken his own life. One evening, when the staff was ready to leave, they had set the alarm and were heading out. Upon opening the door, a man who had been loitering about the property for the past week fell backward into the room. At first they thought he was drunk, but on further examination they saw he had taken his life with a gun. After the police arrived, the staff gave their statements as the medical examiner took custody of the body. As the staff was being released, a detective told the staff to expect a call from the man's family as he had a note in his pocket indicating he wanted to be taken care of at Serenity Shores. But that call never came and that was the last anyone ever heard of him.

The suicide happened just outside the door to the flower room. At the time, that was the room where all the employees entered and exited the building. It was also a perfect holding area for flowers as it had once been the cold storage area for bodies. Having thick walls and an insulated steel door, the room was also soundproof. I came along to Serenity Shores many years later. I didn't know anything about this suicide until one evening when my co-worker, Agnes, pulled me aside.

"You know what week this is, don't you?" she asked. When I replied that I didn't know, she said, "It's that week, the week we all have to be extra careful. The week we really have to look out for ourselves." She then filled me in on what had happened years earlier and said that this week was the anniversary of the week the man was loitering around the property and finally killed himself.

"He comes back every year, during this week, and scares folks; chases them, stuff like that. You have to be really careful. Don't be here alone at night!" Her story didn't thrill me one bit, and I hoped it was one of her occasional goofy rantings. I was wrong.

While locking up late the next evening with Agnes, I was in the front lobby alone. I had heard someone knocking on the windows earlier, but paid no attention to it as we had kids in the area who sometimes liked to play pranks. I heard the outside doorbell ring next to the double glass doors and looked up in that direction. Agnes was nearby, so when she heard me yell her name she came running.

There, pressed up against the glass, stood a crazy-looking man. He stared straight at us with his face pressed against the glass, fingers spread above his head, and dark, messy, shoulder-length hair that seemed to go everywhere. My reaction was to head for the phone and call the police about this unshaven and snaggletoothed individual whom I thought was drunk. Agnes just stood there, calmly turned toward me and said, "Don't bother. When we turn back around, he'll be gone. I just wish he hadn't seen us, that's all."

I was floored by her calm demeanor. She told me again not to call the police.

"It won't do any good," she said. "He won't be any-where around, he never is. That's the guy who shot himself years ago." It wasn't good that he had seen us, though, as now he had a face to focus on. We turned back toward the door and, as she had predicted, he was gone.

Earlier, just before sundown, she had told me to move my car close to the building, under an awning and next to her car. She said he never went near that area, so I was not to park in any other place this week when I was there at night. When we left for the evening, we went out together and paid close attention to our surroundings. We were for-tunate nothing happened.

Two evenings later, I worked again. Agnes couldn't work that evening or maybe she didn't want to. When I pulled into the parking lot, it was packed solid with cars. The closest I could get to the building was near the trash bin more than fifty yards from the back door. I thought about Agnes' warn-ing as I made my way through the sea of cars and into the funeral home; I also reminded myself to move my car later. When I met up with a co-worker, Ted, who was helping with one of the visitations, I asked if he would stay later with me. To my relief, he let me know he would be happy to stay. He lied.

Several times during that busy evening, I checked the parking lot. Each time, all the close spots, including under the awning, remained full. The evening was hectic at both viewings. I never got a chance to check on Ted and his family, and I never got a chance to move my car. When my family and their friends left, I searched the funeral home for Ted—he was nowhere to be found. I had felt nervous all evening, but now also became angry and hurt.

I went through my routine of cleaning and locking up, taking the time to peer out the windows to look for the creepy being from two nights earlier; he didn't appear. I talked myself into thinking that everything would be fine. As I put my fingers on the buttons to set the alarm, I heard grunting noises just outside the door.

I could not see through the door, so I went into a nearby office and looked out the window. I was relieved to see nothing there and thought it must have just been my stomach growling. But I was still frightened and nervous.

I thought about calling my husband and asking him to meet me there, but remembered he was working late that evening. I tried to think of someone else who could come over and came up with zilch. I had gotten worked up again and now had to talk myself into getting out of there. I considered staying the night in the mortuary, but having no idea if the spirit had ever gotten in, I thought staying might be a bad idea.

I pulled myself together while remembering that when the last of the family had left, they were fine. I tried counting back the days to when Agnes had first told me of the suicide spook. I hoped his week was over. I took a deep breath, said a prayer, and told myself again that everything would be fine. I was ready. I set the alarm, walked out the door with my car key poised between fingers and thumb, shut the door while taking a quick look around the area, and began the fifty-yard trek to my car.

Behind me, I heard quick footsteps and grunting. I turned my head and saw he was following me, the creepy man from two nights earlier, with a limping gait and blind determination. I ran toward my car, keys at the ready, praying I wouldn't turn my ankle. He got closer. I wanted to scream, but it stuck in my throat. I had to keep moving as sweat rolled down my face.

I got to my car, rammed the key in the lock, and turned it the wrong direction; the door wouldn't open. I looked back and he was steadily moving toward me. I turned the key again and threw the door open. I jumped inside the car, threw my stuff onto the seat, and slammed and locked the door. I shoved the key into the ignition; the car wouldn't start. He was almost at my car! I turned it over one more time; success, ignition. He was now on the trunk of my car. I screamed as he climbed up onto the roof and made growls that sounded like they came from the pit of Hell.

I threw the car in drive and gunned it. He slid off of the car. I peeled out of the parking lot. Looking in the rearview mirror, I saw he was up and walking dejectedly in the direction of the building. As I watched, he disappeared. There one second—gone the next.

I drove two blocks and realized I was shaking like a leaf. I pulled into a busy grocery store parking lot to gather myself together. Instead, I broke into tears. After having a good cry, I drove home. I didn't sleep that night and not much the next. Every noise had me up and out of bed. I didn't like being alone and was glad I didn't have to go back to work for a while.

I later tried to talk with Agnes about the encounter, but she wanted to hear nothing of it. I was fortunate to not get scheduled during that anniversary week in the following years that I worked at Serenity Shores. Or perhaps the directors who scheduled services and viewings knew better than to schedule during that week. Or maybe business just slowed down. I was never sure.

I was alone in my experience and never shared it with anyone, including my husband, until recently when I forced myself to talk to him about it. He let me know that, had he known what had transpired that evening, he would have encouraged me to quit. After that night, I wouldn't have argued with him one bit.

CHAPTER 11

THE DIRECTORS
STILL AT WORK

In the funeral industry many people have a passion and a calling for their work. Whether a licensed director, a cemeterian, an embalmer, or cremationist, they spend long hours on the job and seek no extra compensation. The results are reward enough. Some of these dedicated individuals have been known to return to their posts after they, too, have needed the expertise and professionalism of their colleagues. In three different funeral homes I've been blessed to work in, we had individual spirits such as these.

At Sherwood Mortuary and Cremation Service, one spirit was that of an embalmer who was quite a noisy fellow. The employees knew him as *our ghost*. No one seemed to be bothered by him, his antics, or his noise, which I found very refreshing. I thought most people would become freaked out knowing there was a spirit in the prep room, but not these folks. They were used to him and ignored his shenanigans. I, on the other hand, having not worked in this home very long, was nervous in the beginning, but I too eventually got used to *our ghost*.

I had been working at Sherwood for about three months when I had my first encounter with *our ghost*. Our prep room had been busy for several days; we were embalming non-stop and almost around the clock. The room had been freshly cleaned, sanitized, and empty for the first time in a week. The crematory retorts were also empty and cooling. It had been an exceptionally busy week and we were greatly appreciative of a little downtime.

I was enjoying the feeling of luxurious calm that had overtaken the entire building as I took my time setting up a chapel for the last of the families. They were due to arrive at any moment to view their loved one for the first time before the public would be allowed to enter.

As I set the last floral arrangement next to the casket, my supervisor ran into the chapel and asked why I had placed a body that was to be cremated on the table for embalming. I had no idea what he was talking about and politely told him so. He went back into the office while mumbling and chuckling. At Sherwood, everyone had a great sense of humor, so I thought this might be one of their fun antics. But since I wasn't sure, I decided to check out the prep room for myself knowing that there hadn't been a body there when I left the room twenty minutes earlier.

As I entered, there was indeed a body on the prep table. On the nearby counter, I found the paperwork for the deceased; this person's final disposition was to be cremation with no embalming. Well, at least I knew that my supervisor hadn't been pulling my leg.

I went into the office where I asked the other directors the same question my supervisor had asked of me. They all responded that since I had been the only person out of the office during the time, I had to have been the one who put it there and could be the one to put it back. Thinking this was part of their quirky sense of humor, I went back to the prep room where I pulled the body off the embalming table and onto a wheeled dressing table. I rolled it through the dressing area, down the long sea-green hallway that led to the building's massive cooler, and ended my trek by placing the body on an empty shelf after wrapping it in a clean, white sheet.

After this workout, I had time to kick back for a few minutes with a cup of coffee and wait for my family to arrive. The remaining staff left for the day, and I became the only living person in the building. I waited patiently.

The family arrived in good spirits and took some private time with their loved one. During the public viewing, Sue, one of the grown daughters of the deceased, walked up to me at the front desk and asked if the ghost's radio in the back room could be turned down.

"The what?" I asked her.

"The ghost's radio," she said nicely. "You know you have a ghost in this building, don't you? Well, he's listening to his radio in some room in the back. Please get him to turn it off because we can hear it through the wall."

I walked into the chapel area with Sue and, sure enough, the sound of a radio could be heard through the wall. I apologized and let the family know I would take care of it immediately.

Walking cautiously through several doors and hallways to get to the back rooms, I followed the music; hard rock from the seventies. I moved farther into the core of the building, thinking the music sounded like it was coming from the prep room, yet I had shut down that room completely when I relocated the body earlier.

I walked through four rooms and two hallways to get to the prep room. With each doorway I walked through, the music got louder. My walking slowed, and I became more cautious, not knowing what to expect in the next room or hallway. Funeral homes usually have a labyrinth of rooms and this one was no exception. Of course, it didn't help that every room and hallway was dark with not even a security light to gently light my way.

As I entered the last hallway before the entrance to the prep room, I stopped short. There, off to my right, down at the end of the long, narrow, storage corridor for cremains awaiting someone to claim them, were two red, glowing eyes. I felt my heart enter my throat and stressed squeals tried to get out of my mouth. I couldn't breathe. I couldn't remember where the light switches were and frantically rubbed my hands on the cold, lumpy brick wall while the music pounded close by. My feet wanted to run back the way I'd come, but they seemed to be glued to the floor. With my heart pounding loudly in my ears I located the switch and turned on the lights.

My eyes were focused toward the red, glowing eyes, which now proved to be nothing more than the indicator lights for the private security door at the opposite end of the hall. I started to laugh after catching my breath and collecting myself, but this laughter was not to last long.

I came to my senses and shook off the lingering adrenaline of the last few seconds. I still had my mission to accomplish and get that radio turned off. I was now certain the sound came from the prep room on the other side of the door in front of me. The music was deafening and I could barely hear myself think.

I placed my hand on the door handle and cautiously pushed the door open. I expected the room to be dark since that's the way I'd left it, but bright light flooded out of the room. I looked around and saw no one in the room. I went over to the radio across the room and turned it off. With the sudden silence, I noticed more background noise; the aspiration sink was running and the exhaust fans were turned on.

"Now I know I didn't leave *these* on," I said to myself. I stood in the bleach-laced clean of the cold, clinical prep room, scratching my head and trying to figure out what had happened. I began to wonder if one of my co-workers had snuck in while I was with the family in the chapel. I tried being logical even though unnerved. I laughed at the thought of my colleagues going to this length to pull a prank.

I went back to my family and all went well for another thirty minutes, until just before the family was ready to start their private service.

Sue approached me once again and said, "Hon? Your ghost is at it again. The radio's back on. You may want to unplug it this time. Okay?"

I went through the trek a lot quicker this time and paid no attention to the glowing red lights at the end of the last hallway. The radio was indeed on again and just as loud. I thought Sue might be correct about a ghost in the room. I was irritated now, so after I unplugged the radio, I moved it to the trash bucket next to the door.

"There, smart aleck, leave it there and leave it off until these people are outta here—if you *are* a ghost!" I said. I left the room after turning off the lights and closing the door. I had crossed the hallway and was shutting the adjoining hallway door when I heard the sound of someone hitting their fist on the metal embalming table followed by a man's voice yelling *"No!"*

I stopped dead in my tracks. I didn't know whether to run away, go back in there and have it out with who or whatever spoke, or go back and take care of my family. I wanted to do all three, but settled on doing my job of taking care of the family and quickly made my way back to the chapel.

Upon my return, the family was ready to begin their service. Sue waved to me from the front of the room and gave me a questioning signal similar to the action of pulling a cord out of a wall. I nodded to her that this had been done. She wiped her brow, mouthed "Whew," and gave me the thumbs-up.

All went well during the service until near the very end. I started to hear seventies music again, low but audible. Sue heard it, too. She got up and walked solemnly to the back of the room.

"You get back there fast," she whispered. "Your ghost is gonna crank it up again. Just ask him, this time, to keep it down for us. I'll talk with you later. Now, move it; run!"

I knew this was exactly what I needed to do. The music became louder as I got closer to the prep room. I didn't have time to think about being scared or the luxury of remembering that I'd unplugged the radio and sat it across the room. I didn't think about the bang and the man's voice. I just ran through the maze into the core of the building.

I grabbed the door handle and it was ice cold this time. It made me draw back and utter "Ouch!" This was enough to bring me back to full consciousness about the prior happenings. I cautiously opened the door, using my jacket as insulation between my hand and the paddle. The air inside the prep room was now ice cold. The lights were on, and the radio was not only on but steadily getting louder. It was also back on the counter yet still unplugged.

I wondered what I should do, and then remembered what Sue had suggested. I pulled myself together and decided to speak kindly to the spirit. Even though my voice, hands, and knees were shaking, I had to give it a try.

"Hey, spirit-guy, please, would you mind turning off the music?" I asked. "There's a family in the chapel finishing up their service. When they're gone, you can turn the tunes back on, no problem. Please?" The room went silent. I heard nothing except the sound of my breathing and my heartbeat. I thanked the spirit and walked back to the chapel on wobbly legs.

The family milled about after their service. Many let me know how good the deceased looked, along with asking what all the noise was in the back room. I told them we'd had some electrical glitches in the building and were looking into the cause to have them repaired.

Sue came up to me and took me aside for a little chat. She told me she could walk into any building and know that ghosts were there. She couldn't bring herself to communicate with them, but knew that I could, already had, and would be asked to do so again in the future.

Sue informed me that I would get to know the spirits and energies of the building quickly. She had attended a few services at Sherwood and knew several spirits were here that would reveal themselves to me, more than to the other employees, as I was willing to listen.

Once everyone left, the building now felt calm and serene. I was locking up the oversized double glass swinging doors of the front lobby when my cell phone rang. It was my supervisor.

"You know that body that was on the embalming table, the one you moved to the cooler?" he asked. When I replied yes, he continued, "Go get it back out and put it back on the embalming table again. I've got to embalm it at dawn. Seems his children found a letter from him telling them that he never wanted to be cremated. I've just done up their new contract and they want a service tomorrow evening. Will you get him out for me and ready to go for the morning?"

Okay, no problem. I had to laugh at the evening as a whole. Oh well, I had everything locked up and cleaned for the night; I just had to retrieve that body again.

I proceeded into the lobby, through a darkened hallway, through an interior walk-in closet, into the dressing area, and into the hallway leading toward the cooler; another labyrinth. The cooler at Sherwood was a huge walk-in unit capable of holding more than twenty bodies. I had left the body on a nearby shelf wearing the clothing he was wearing in death and wrapped in a sheet. I slid open the huge double-thick, insulated door and couldn't find the body where I'd left it. I looked on every shelf and couldn't have missed it as there were no other bodies in the cooler.

I closed the cooler door and slowly walked through the hall, through the dressing room, and into the prep room. I stopped dead in my tracks.

There, on the embalming table, was the body I'd been looking for. Not only was the body there, it was undressed with its dignity fully preserved. The entire body was respectfully covered with a fresh, bleached, white sheet from head to toe and ready for embalming. The thermostat in the room had been adjusted for the preservation and acclimation of the body.

After I shook off my amazement and realized everything was good, I had to prove a few things to myself. I wanted to know how the radio had played while not being plugged into the wall.

"Batteries, that's it." I whispered. I took the thing apart; there were no batteries. In fact, there hadn't been batteries in that radio for a long time as I found a lot of dust in the battery compartment.

I finished putting the rest of the building to bed for the night. It had gotten very late by this time and I was grateful to have the next two days off. Before I turned off the front lights and set the alarm, I went to the prep room to check on the deceased one last time. He was still there and ready for embalming. I plugged the radio back in and made sure it was off.

Just prior to turning out the light, I thankfully said, "Whoever you are, I sure do thank you for getting this person set up on the table; nice job."

I turned off the light, exited the room, and quietly closed the door. As I walked away, I heard the light switch click back on in the prep room and a male voice say "you're welcome" along with the sound of medical instruments being moved about. I was too tired to go back and investigate any further.

When I returned to work after my weekend, my supervisor took me aside and thanked me for preparing the body for him.

"You set the instruments out just like Jack did, though," he said. "That's creepy and anal. You must be one picky person."

I replied I've been known to be picky and asked who Jack was.

"Jack used to work here about twelve years ago," he told me. "He loved working here. We liked him a lot, even though he played his radio full blast."

"Why isn't he still here, then?" I asked.

"Oh, don't you know? Jack died in a motorcycle accident. He'd still be working here if he hadn't."

Apparently, Jack *is* still working there.

At Chapel of the Briar, another funeral home where I did some substitution work, they also had a very dedicated employee who had loved working there while he was alive.

While waiting on families or making arrangements, we often heard music coming from the back areas near the prep room or in the inner offices. Sometimes, we heard whistling coming from various areas of the home. Doors would open and shut, lights turned on and off, and we came into work in the mornings to find music playing on the CD player.

I never had any direct interactions with this spirit. The staff all knew who he was, though. He was a dear funeral director who had passed suddenly due to a heart attack while performing one of his favorite duties: embalming.

Even in death, he is the only employee allowed to play the radio or CD player in the prep room or office. This spirit is well loved and very dear to all at Chapel of the Briar.

At my favorite funeral home, Serenity Shores, we had one interesting character that I feel will forever be on the job. He is a strong spirit with a great sense of humor, kindness, and fairness. Many at this mortuary have seen him, and several have tried, unsuccessfully, to photograph him. Many acknowledge his presence, yet no one knows his name. We just called him the Director.

While many have seen him, some have also spoken to and interacted with him without knowing it. Families have come to the funeral home to make arrangements for their loved one, and the Director has greeted them. They've been kindly and warmly welcomed, then shown to a private arrangement room to relax. They are given packets of information to look at before meeting with *their* director, are offered fresh coffee and cookies or donuts, and informed that someone will be with them shortly. Finally, they shake the hand of this kind and beautiful man while never knowing he's in spirit.

Nearly everyone who spent any time in the building eventually crossed paths with the Director, even the children of the employees. One little girl, Katy, would meet her mom at the funeral home every week and spend the afternoon. Katy would quietly play in or near the front desk and was extremely well behaved for a five-year-old.

Many times, Katy's mom and I would walk into the front lobby and hear the child chatting with someone. She would look around the wall, then wave and smile at someone at the end of the hallway. If we were lucky, we caught him out of the corner of our eyes. Usually we asked her who she had been speaking to or waving at. Her answer was always the same, "The nice, tall man in the black suit with the pretty smile."

We occasionally saw the nice, tall man in the black suit in full view just as Katy did. When I first started working at Serenity Shores, I bumped into him when we were both walking through a doorway. I reached for the door leading into the main corridor when it opened on its own from the other side; he walked into the hall I was walking out of. I came face to face with one of the most handsome men I'd ever laid my eyes on.

At more than six feet tall, his dark, violet-brown eyes seemed to peer into my soul with compassion and strength. His thick, dark lashes matched his perfectly coiffed hair that had just a hint of grey at the temples. The tailored black suit he wore fit a set of shoulders that yearned to have a woman's head resting upon them. He smelled nice, too, and left me speechless.

"Be careful of this door," he stated with a voice that could hypnotize a woman by just reading the phone book. "You never know when someone's gonna plow through it." He gave me a smile, patted my shoulder, and walked on in the direction I had just come from. I said nothing as I watched him walk elegantly down the hall.

When I went into the office later, I asked who the new good-looking guy was. The other employees looked at me and asked, "What new guy?" I described the man who I had bumped into. One of the women just laughed. Another said that I was seeing things and they didn't have an employee who looked like that. When I asked other employees about him, I got the same oddly evasive remarks.

One of my co-workers finally told me I had run into the Director. He was someone who may have worked there years before, but nobody knew who he was. My boss confirmed they had all seen him from time to time, and some employees were frightened of him and wanted him to go away. He also told me that most funeral homes have dead directors wandering about. Many people who enter this profession apparently never leave.

Funeral directors should show the family compassion, confidence, and trust along with a tasteful touch of humor for a dose of stress-relief. For one family in particular, the Director shone in all these areas. And no one realized how much he was enjoying himself as much as I.

This incident happened when I was running the show as a favor for another director who had become ill. The service was a private one that the family had kept secret from us as they had made what they referred to as *special arrangements*. We were informed that these arrangements included a film crew along with a unique theologian.

The family arrived and spent some private time with their loved one. A girl, barely out of her teens, wearing Goth clothing and makeup entered the chapel's lobby about thirty minutes after the family arrived. In her black chunky shoes, black bat-winged skirt, black leggings, and spider-embroidered purple and silver blouse, she wandered about the lobby as if she was lost.

She finally walked up to me and introduced herself, "Like, my name is Angel, and I'm, like, here to, like, work for the family of this really awesome dead dude. So, like, where can I like set up my stuff?"

"And what stuff would that be?" I asked the Goth Valley Girl.

"I, like, need a spot that, like, has a really clear view of the dead dude in the coffin," she answered while popping her pink bubble gum. "I'm gonna, like, set up my cameras and stuff so I can get really good ghost activity. Like, I am totally for sure there are ghosts in this entire church place, and I'm gonna get proof of the life-after-death thing for the dude's family. This is like gonna be, like, totally awesome."

My senses reeled with what they needed to process all at once. I had been told to expect anything, but a Goth-Ghost-Hunting-Valley-Girl was the furthest thing from my mind. I prayed that God would give me strength for this one.

While she was speaking to me, she pulled a small hand-held device out of a maroon velvet bag and started fiddling with its dials and buttons. A member of the family approached us and let me know Angel was there at their request and had been approved. The family member was speaking with Angel and giving me a quick synopsis of what would be transpiring that evening when I saw him, in full form, for the second time in as many months.

The Director walked out of our clergy meditation room behind the two women. He was there, all six foot three inches of him, in a beautifully tailored black suit and tie, immaculate white shirt with French cuffs and gold cuff links. His dark hair with slight graying at the temples and dark violet-brown eyes were the perfect accompaniment to his beautiful, slightly tanned skin. He looked in my direction, gave me a wave and a wink, and produced the warmest of smiles. He also held his finger up to his lips indicating I should keep quiet and not mention him.

He moved closer to the family member and Angel as they continued chatting about this wonderful piece of equipment that was so sensitive it could "like, pick up ghost energy from, like, anywhere in, like, the immediate area." As they espoused the virtues of this wonderful item, the Director looked at Angel quizzically. He covered his mouth to stop his laughter.

Angel continued to fiddle with the handheld item and stated, "Like, this little beauty will totally get any ghostly apparition's energy in the vicinity. It's totally awesome!" The Director lost it and was forced to go back into the meditation room to laugh, which he made sound like a cough. At this time I could see the gauge on the "totally awesome little beauty," and it was registering zero with a real spirit not fifteen feet away.

The two people in front of me heard the Director coughing in the meditation room and asked if my associate would be okay. I, too, was having difficulty holding it together, but I kept my composure and assured them he would be fine.

"I certainly wouldn't want him to, like, die or something. Gaaa…" Angel stated. I heard another spell of coughing from the meditation room.

"I'm sure he'll be fine." I replied while wondering if I could also make laughter sound like a cough if I ducked into the ladies' room.

I showed Angel where she could set up her equipment so that she had a clear view of the casket and wasn't in the way of the family's clergy. Angel interrupted me to tell me *she* was the clergy.

"Yeah I, like, get the ghosts of the dead people on film and other recordings and stuff. Then I, like, transport them into the next life and get them to, like, go into the light. It's sooo totally awesome to see; you'll have to, like, watch. It's, like, as if the whole room begins to float."

As she brought in her thermal camera and a temperature gauge, I didn't see the Director anywhere and thought he was done for the evening. But as Angel checked the setup and calibration on the cameras and other equipment she'd brought in, which included a laptop computer, the Director appeared once again. He walked up to the casket as directors normally do to check on the condition of the deceased. He then walked over to the family and spoke with them for a few minutes, offering his condolences while holding their hands comfortingly.

Goth-Ghost-Hunting-Valley-Girl was so busy talking about her equipment and how fantastic it and she were that she never bothered to look at the monitors. While I could plainly see the Director, her camera and other equipment did not see or detect him at all. In the camera, it looked as if the family was speaking to thin air. Angel commented on how nice-looking my associate was, but still wouldn't look at the camera or monitors. I was not about to point anything out to her either, as I was having some fun, too.

I had returned to the lobby and was taking care of guests when Angel let out a high-pitched squeal. I ran into her area from my post in the lobby to see if she was all right. Family and friends had flocked to her side.

She caught what she referred to as a *manifestation* on what she kept incorrectly referring to as the *coffin* and was playing back the images for all to see. I viewed it also and knew immediately what she had gotten. The temperature of the room was chilly, the body was cold, and the casket was made of steel, which stays cool. The people were warm bodies, hot from coming in from outside and highly emotional as they came up to the casket to pay their respects, often leaning on the casket. Her thermal equipment had picked up the image of hands upon the casket where several grieving people had touched it, took their hands off of the casket, and walked away. Within seconds, the image disappeared as the metal returned to the temperature of the room. She swore to everyone within shouting distance that ghosts and angels had their hands all over the deceased and the *coffin*.

As the evening wore on, so did my patience. The Director popped in from time to time, purposefully walking in front of the detection devices, which continually didn't react as they allegedly were supposed to when a spirit was around, and then politely walk out of the area.

I had to keep a close eye on Angel as she felt it was her duty to go into the private back room areas and *release* the ghosts she felt were trapped there. I was forced to lock up the other rooms in the building as she felt it was also her right to view bodies in the cooler so she could properly send them into the light.

My patience was just about at its end when she began her preparation for her *passing over ritual ceremony*. I do not deny anyone their own beliefs or begrudge them their need to worship in their own way, but it is against the law to defile a corpse or have too much fire in a public building. Angel had brought a case of one hundred candles and intended to put them everywhere, including on the deceased. I informed her and the family about fire codes and the combustibility of formaldehyde. She was terribly disappointed, but the family understood. I permitted her to light a dozen candles that were secured to stands of various heights; I also had a fire extinguisher near the casket and one with me, just in case.

Nearly thirty minutes later, while still standing at my post in the lobby and keeping watch over Angel's endless ritual gyrations, laughter began emanating from the men's room. The laughter was infectious and lightened the energy of the entire area. I wanted to join in, but had to remain stoic. The laughter quieted and became a beautifully deep, masculine voice with a breathless, yet jovial, lilt saying, "Oh—my—gosh! This has been fun, but I've gotta go. Catch ya later." I then heard a toilet flush.

I waited for several minutes for the gentleman to make his exit, but he didn't. I had been standing by the only exit of the men's room the entire time and no one had gone past me. I went into the room to see if the man was okay, but found the room empty. I knew that it had been the Director I'd heard speak, as well as laugh.

The family and their ghost hunter, with all of her stuff, finally left. We never found out if she had recorded any validating evidence on her special equipment. But I've had plenty of validation that spirits exist; no fancy equipment needed. Through paying attention with an open mind, a dose of patience, and a sense of humor, I've received knowledge, truth, assistance, and a few laughs to boot. What gifts to have been given by these wonderful directors who are still on the job and apparently loving it.

CHAPTER 12

WHEN THEY MOVE
YOU BY MOVING

After attaining my degree in Mortuary Science while working full time and also passing my National Board Exam,
I began my one-year internship to become a licensed
embalmer. That year seemed to fly by as I was able to
embalm well over my required amount of bodies while also
arranging funerals for many other people at their time of
need. When people find out I am a mortician and embalm
bodies, I am often asked many questions by curious minds
who want to know fact from fiction.

One of the first and most frequent questions asked is if
a body is able to move on its own post-mortem. Yes, a body
can move after death, but not in the way movies, books, and
television depict movement. I have never seen a body sit up
in the morgue or on a bed shortly after death. I have been

told, by some morgue attendants and one nurse, that the body may appear to sit up, but not to a full seated position. A body may move a bit due to final muscle spasms, but it would not be a very large movement that would resemble a sit up or a twist of the torso.

Many things I know from personal experience. Bodies can seem to vomit. This action is called purging, and the fluids exuded are referred to as *purge*. Bodily fluids take the path of least resistance and often exit through the mouth, but they will exit through any available orifice including pores and ducts. Many things working together can make a body purge, in tandem and alone. Gas buildup from the normal and natural process of decomposition, causing pressure internally, is often the main cause of purge, but the cause of death and weather conditions, including the temperature of the room, are also factors that contribute to expulsion of fluid by a dead body. How a body is moved or transported as well as a bad embalming job can also cause it to purge.

Bodies can seem to moan or sing post-mortem. This is due to the last exhalation of breath moving out of the lungs. Though people may be sitting with their loved one at the time of the death happening, it can take more than an hour for the last bit of air to make its way out of the lungs. This air moves past the vocal chords and causes the moaning or singing that an inexperienced person may notice—and that person may get a bit unnerved by a dead body making sounds.

Embalmers often cause a body to wheeze, whistle, or sing during the embalming process while they remove body cavity fluids. How the air moves during the interior aspiration procedure is dependent upon how clean we can get the inside of the torso—and believe me when I say the cleaner, the better.

Bodies may also twist, just slightly, during cremation. They neither sit all the way up nor scream. If a body moves at all, it slightly contorts due to the muscle tissue and ligaments drying out, causing them to contract during the cremation process; similar to a leaf drying and curling after falling from a tree.

There is also an interesting physical phenomenon called *spontaneous rigor mortis*. This happens when a person dies during a very high-stress situation, such as suicide, a traumatic death, or death on a battlefield. Natural rigor mortis sets in on a deceased body anywhere from an hour to as long as twelve hours post-mortem, depending upon many factors externally and internally with the body. It will also fixate in whatever position it is lying in during this process, but is fairly easy to manipulate out of its pose. In the case of spontaneous rigor mortis, the body locks into the position it was in at the time of death. This is where we get the term *death grip*. These bodies can be a challenge to get to relax and may have a type of memory of their positioning even after manipulation.

A person who seeks their own demise by holding a gun in their hand and pulling the trigger will often stay locked in the position in which they die. The arm is usually moved away from the shooting point due to the recoil of the weapon, but the hand itself will still look as if it is holding the gun, even if the gun has jumped out of the hand during the firing.

A soldier who dies on the battlefield under the high-stress situation of battle will often be found in the same position that they were in while firing their weapon or preparing to make a thrust. This form of rigor is the hardest to work out of the body and extra care must be taken with the body to not cause further damage.

During the process that embalmers call *breaking up the rigor*, we put the body through extensive massage and manual manipulation of the limbs, fingers, toes, neck, jaw, and fingertips. We do this to work out the rigor and have maximum diffusion of the arterial fluid. But even with all the work we do to a body in spontaneous rigor, the body often makes a darn good attempt at returning to the original position of death. Embalmers have to work especially hard to get the body to relax, which is necessary so it will rest with a natural appearance in the casket.

During the actual embalming process, when we literally relax the rigor and work the body so that the embalming fluids will penetrate more thoroughly, sometimes the body will still move. I have worked the muscles and ligaments of the arms, gotten them to relax, and still received a hug that I wasn't ready for. The first time a body part moves, it is quite a shock, but embalmers get used to the slight movements and know they are normal things that bodies in this state do.

During one embalming, I was working on the body of a person who had passed away due to an automobile collision. I had the deceased's arms out to the side so that I could work on the chest and belly areas. While I was standing on the left side of the body and working on the belly area, the left arm slowly curled back in. I did not notice the movement due to being totally engrossed in locating the iliac and femoral arteries so I could properly embalm the person's legs.

When I finally noticed the movement, the arm had drawn back in toward the side of the body and I felt the arm gently encircling my waist. Apparently, the body wished to still hold onto the steering wheel. As I was in a positive mood, I looked at the face of the deceased and said, "Hello, there. Please, we have not been properly introduced! Keep your arm out there now. I have a lot of work to do. Thank you kindly." I gently yet firmly moved the arm back out to its stable position and continued with my work.

Occasionally, a body will pass gas, and many wonder if the flatulence is audible from a dead body. The answer is *sometimes*, and it depends upon where the gas is emitting from and the pressure behind it. Usually, a touch of purge will accompany this flatulence so embalmers try to plug the leaks should they occur.

Not only do we embalmers look at the body, we also listen to it. I personally have been witness to bodies that seemed to belch and pass gas, those that looked like they are breathing due to gas building up in the chest, and others that appeared to be snoring due to small amounts of gas coming out of a closed mouth. This shouldn't happen if the body has been embalmed properly, but sometimes it still does no matter how much time and effort is taken. Embalmers don't know for sure how a body is going to react to embalming; we rely on our knowledge, training, and expertise while sometimes being forced to hope for the best.

Up to this point, everything I've mentioned has been explainable through science and the natural occurrences of decomposition and putrefaction. That doesn't mean every movement of dead bodies is scientifically explainable, though.

Sometimes, I have felt the spirit of the deceased present and wanting to lend a helping hand. Many things have happened that validate this for me.

For instance, many times women have relaxed their hands so that I could apply their nail polish properly and make them look beautiful. The first time this happened was with the body of an elderly woman who had horrible arthritis throughout her body. Her hands were so gnarled that it was impossible to get them to relax. Even seasoned embalmers couldn't get her hands to lie in a relaxed position using massage, manipulation, and weighting. I looked at her hands and tried massaging and manipulating them myself, yet obtained no better results. Her poor fingers still had the full arthritic lumps and curl, yet her nails had to be manicured and polished.

I did not know what else to do, so I figured it wouldn't hurt to ask if she might be able to assist me. I took a deep breath, closed my eyes, and spoke to her. I cradled her hands in mine and said a prayer while gently smoothing her fingers. All of a sudden, as if she heard me, her hands relaxed in mine and hung naturally. They had also lost their arthritic appearance and looked young again. When I raised her hands to elevate them onto a towel, her fingers laid gracefully as if she was in the manicurist's chair. I gave that woman the best manicure I had ever done in my life.

I know that her spirit came in to assist for a few minutes. I feel she knew I was trying to work on her while she also appreciated the effort and importance that I placed on this somewhat mundane task. The energy in the room changed from chaotic and noisy to calm and peaceful. There was also the scent of perfume in the air when no one had used any. This was all the evidence I needed.

I have also had cases where I have been asked to apply the makeup on women whose families could not provide a photo for me to use as a guide. When the time would come to do the final cosmetizing, I would close my eyes, hold their hand, ask them for help on doing their makeup, and say a prayer. When I would complete the job, I often found myself standing back, with tears in my eyes, in awe of how beautiful these dearly departed women had become. The women's families always commented and sometimes asked if I had seen her before as the effect was so accurate and natural. Every woman has her own style and method of makeup application; I could never have completed their look without their dearly departed help.

Dressing the deceased is another time when I have felt the deceased return to lend a final helping hand. In most cases, dressing the deceased takes about ten minutes. There are times, however, when the body does not want to cooperate and I've been forced to cut the clothing down the back and prove that one size does fit all. When I struggle with a body, I go into action with my ritual, and lo and behold, the body begins to work with me and ends up looking sharp and snazzy.

Moving in any way is not something we often think about in regards to the dead, but we do wonder. When we know more about the dead and the life hereafter, I think we'll agree they are definitely our spirited dead.

CHAPTER 13

DID I JUST SEE
A SHADOW?

Peter Pan lost his and tried to stick it back onto his feet with a bar of soap after he'd found it in the nursery. My cats liked to play with theirs when they were kittens. Depending upon the angle of the sun, we may find that we have more than one when we're outside. I'm talking about shadows. Simple, ordinary, run-of-the-mill shadows. We all know them, see them all over, and are used to them and pay them no mind; that is, until they cross our paths, alone.

Many people notice what are referred to as *shadow people*. Numerous discussions over the Internet and on radio talk shows are about this phenomenon. I've seen shadow people ever since I was a child, so they aren't anything new to me. Even though I've seen them, I'm not too thrilled when I do. This is one phenomenon that gives me the

creeps. I think that's because most of the ones I've encountered are sneaky or too bold and often have red, glowing
eyes.

We've all seen them, either out of the corner of our eyes
or straight on. They seem to be appearing with more frequency to many more people, which accounts for the great
amount of discussion and theories about them. There are
almost as many thoughts about shadow people as there are
folks discussing them. Some think they are demons, angels,
or djinn, while others think that they are nothing more than
figments of our imagination or maladies of our ocular orbits.
All these opinions and theories are correct.

Many folks who are a bit more scientific feel that the
shadow people are from different time periods or moving
through time. The increase in sightings is attributed to bio-
matter or a thinner layer between the dimensions, provable
through the theories surrounding quantum physics. People
who look at the metaphysical side feel that shadow people
are trapped, lost, or doomed souls. These are correct as
well. The thing about shadow people is, just like with any
other manifestation, it depends upon the situation. Each is
as unique as we are.

I wondered for a long time, why shadow people would
show up at funerals. One in particular showed up and
drifted down the aisle during certain services. I never knew
what to make of it. It moved past me on several occasions while I stood in the lobby of a funeral home chapel
or church vestibule. It drifted gracefully, like an elegant,
sooty cloud of smoke, but with direction and purpose. As it

passed, I could smell the odor of dust or mustiness. Neither scent was offensive like the smell of decomposition would be; it was just dry and dusty, sometimes with a touch of forest mold thrown in.

Occasionally, I did not see the shadow, but smelled the odor. When the scent was present and the shadow wasn't, I was fairly certain that it was somewhere in the room, whether I could see it or not.

The first time I noticed this particular shadow was at the funeral of a person whose family I had serviced far too often. This poor family was emotionally broken and had brought many of their loved ones to me by way of the matriarch of the family, Agatha. I grew to dread seeing Agatha get out of her car in the parking lot. She came to me with eleven of her relatives and close friends who had passed on.

At the last service, the shadow appeared twice; the first time in the chapel itself and the second in the cemetery. During the service in the chapel and just prior to going to the cemetery, all the family and friends were sitting quietly with their heads bowed in prayer. From the lobby it drifted down the main chapel aisle to the casket. It turned slowly toward Agatha, drifted directly in front of her, stopped, looked down at her, bowed its head, and disappeared. No one noticed the shadow or its movements except for me. I was astonished and concerned, wondering why this spirit, this shadow, had chosen to plague this poor woman.

Later that morning, after we'd moved the service to the cemetery, I observed the shadow again. This time it circled the crowd that had gathered around the casket as we prepared to lower Agatha's loved one into the ground. Once again, when all heads were bowed in prayer the shadow entity appeared, circled the group, stood for a second at the foot of the casket, bowed its head toward the deceased this time, and disappeared. Now, in the light of day, the shadow vaguely resembled the Reaper, but without the stereotypical scythe.

At the family's request, I stayed with the body at the cemetery until the closing was complete, which is the term for when the casket is completely lowered, the vault is secured, and the earth filled in. I had time to think about the events of the day. I remembered that Reapers are also Angels, and they are doing the job they were meant to do. I hoped that their job was done when it came to this family. Maybe he was stopping by to make sure he was finished with them for a long while; I pray so.

After I left the funeral business, I still kept in touch with various colleagues who remain my friends to this day. On one occasion, I was chatting with Carmen, a close friend who is still employed at one of my favorite funeral homes, Serenity Shores. Carmen is also sensitive when it comes to spirits and told me that several employees were getting nervous about the shadows. They were increasing in number throughout the building. The shadows appear in the corridors and offices, move in and out via the ceiling, and even appear to come up out of the ground. Carmen feels the other employees will get used to them and quit talking about them, like they do with the other spirits, and eventually ignore them.

Carmen sees them in the largest southern chapel and the largest parlor area. She sees a variety of them and told me she has witnessed ones that are smoky and wispy; ones that are shadow-like; and others that are solid black, with and without form. Some are human in shape while others are unidentifiable.

More and more shadow animals are appearing, too. They're of many varieties, including rabbits, house cats, deer, birds, and snakes. They play in the chapels, appear in the meditation gardens, and scamper down the corridors. Some of the cat-like ones have rubbed themselves against her leg while she's working.

Then there are the shadows that appear as clouds *inside* the building. I first saw this type of shadow in the prep room at Sherwood Mortuary and Cremation Service after setting up a body to be embalmed. I had begun the early preparation of the body and left the room to let the body rest and acclimate to the room's temperature. When I returned, a huge, sooty, black shadowy cloud hung over the body; it hovered and churned like a storm at sea. I wondered if the crematory was smoking or the after-burner on the retort had stopped working. Being the wise-ass I can sometimes be, instead of calling the crematory manager, I yelled at the swirling, sooty cloud and told it to get away from my dead guy. It moved as if it were looking toward me and drifted in my direction. That'll teach me to be mouthy with a shadow entity.

I backed up and banged into the door, which abruptly slammed, barring my way out of the room. At that point, I could scream loudly, slip to the floor and whimper, or I could stand there and behave as if I'd done this a hundred times before; in other words, fake it. Brilliant me decided to stand my ground and bluff it away. I had no idea what I was doing.

As the sooty cloud got closer to my face and farther away from the body it became wispier, not as defined, and thinner.

"Hey, you heard me," I said out loud. "Get away from my dead guy. Now!" And, it did. It turned around and went through the door that led toward the crematory. It acted curious, but did as it was told.

Obviously, all spirits, entities, and ghosts are *not* out to frighten us. We need to take that into consideration when we encounter them, no matter where or how they show up; even on painted walls.

At Serenity Shores, we rarely used a room that's connected to one of the smaller chapels. The area is a private space for a small family to sit by themselves if they feel particularly overwrought and need extra privacy. Not only does the little room have pews for the family, it also has its own private restroom and a couch. We kept the sliding wall of the room, which separates it from the chapel, closed because most people don't even like to walk in or through the room.

Even though it's a wonderful and comfortable little room, people don't like it because there is the figure of a man, in shadow, on the white brick wall. I painted that wall twice while I worked there, using two coats of paint each time. The wall looked very nice and we thought the figure was gone. But the form of the man kept coming back. We tried to ignore the shadow man and hoped the families wouldn't notice. But each family would let us know it was spooky to see this shadow of a tall man on the wall. We had difficulties when someone who had been to our home before would return. They would pull us aside to inquire why that wall hadn't been painted. Sometimes a family member could tell the wall had been painted and we had a problem convincing them it was nothing special.

I tried to take digital photos of this wall, but had no luck. With the naked eye, people can see a tall shadow figure of a man. With the eye of a camera, nothing appears.

Shadow entities, people, and animals come in all shapes, sizes, densities, and intelligences. I have no certain thoughts as to why shadow people, in general, are on the increase. Only time will tell.

CHAPTER 14

ASHES TO ASHES, THEY'RE NOT JUST DUST

Many humorous things have been said to me when people find out I'm a mortician, including, "I bet people are just dying to meet you" and "Grabbed yourself a cold one today?"

Then, there are the things pertaining to cremating, like, "Hey, that's a hot one!" or "Gonna be cookin' with gas today?" Believe it or not, I enjoy these little quips; they make me smile.

Crematory humor isn't as common as mortuary humor; I guess that's because cremation is so final and irreversible. Cremation is unique when it's done right. Many people in the funeral industry perform cremations very well. My hat is off in tribute to these talented individuals, especially those who perform cremations with the utmost reverence, dignity, and respect. Unfortunately, I'm not one of them. Not because I'm not good at it or because I'm not allowed to perform them; I simply cannot bring myself to do them.

When I was taking classes to earn my degree, I had the opportunity to take an extra course in cremation. I took it thinking I would increase my value to any funeral home. I thought, *Nothing to it*, until I performed my first one.

At some point during most cremations, the body must be repositioned. The temperature at which a body is cremated is about 1600 degrees Fahrenheit. This high heat is necessary for everything to, basically, turn to dust. When the retort door is lifted, one is witness to what Hades might look like: the blinding flames, the acrid smell, the roaring sound, and the extreme heat. Even at five to eight feet away, depending upon the length of the repositioning rod, one must wear welders' gloves to prevent getting burned by the transition of heat moving up the rod. To most individuals, seeing this would be an awesome vision. To me, it was a vision all right; I just can't say it was awesome.

In a past life, I perished during World War II. I know that, in some way, my past self was forced into doing *clean up* of the *evidence*, but I didn't know how until the day I performed that first cremation. When I lifted the retort door, I was pulled backward from within my soul and whoever I was during WWII came forward. I had to work hard to control the past-self and control my body. My legs trembled, my arms ached, and my back tensed. My body began to sweat profusely; my past-self fought me for control of my body. He wanted to slam the retort door shut and run away. My jaw ached from controlling a silent scream. Even though my hand was over my mouth, an observer standing close by told me he heard me utter something in a language he couldn't understand.

After that first cremation, I had my cremation certification and then my license in hand. Too bad I won't use them, but at least I have been honored to assist with many cremations. I can perform any task required during the cremation as long as it does not deal with fire.

I was very respectful and meticulous about handling the remains, before and after cremating. I often stayed late to process and package the cremains—which is the proper term for the cremated remains, not "ashes"—especially if we had several sets to process or if I knew a family was coming early to pick up their loved one. When I spent time alone in the crematory, I was never cold or bored or ever completely alone either.

One evening, I sat quietly in the crematory, reading a magazine and waiting for the cremains to cool enough to process. They were almost ready, having cooled to a chilly 600 degrees. Separating the crematory operation from the rest of the building was a large, heavy fire door, eight feet high by six feet wide and at least three inches thick. I couldn't see the door because the retorts blocked the view, but I could hear it when it opened and closed because it made a unique sound. As I sat in the crematory, patiently waiting for the cremains to cool, I heard that door open and close. Then I heard footsteps moving around the retorts.

I felt nothing out of the ordinary and thought one of the employees had returned.

The footsteps moved around the room, stopped, moved some more, and then stopped again as if someone were looking for something. I had the lights on in my immediate area, but I couldn't see the area of the room where the sound was coming from. I threw on the switch illuminating the entire area and saw nothing, but I heard a moan that sounded as if a person was reacting to a bright light after being in the dark. I felt like saying "Sorry!" but I could not see anyone to say sorry to.

"Hello? Who's there? Where are you?" I sheepishly called out. All that came back was the sound of the footsteps and an occasional sniffling.

As I looked into the area where the person had to be standing in, I knew I was in the room with a spirit. I decided to continue waiting with the cremains, which were now down to 500 degrees, and thought perhaps this spirit had allergies because the sniffling got more frequent.

After a little while, whoever it was walked back toward the door and I again heard the door open and close. The cremains were cool enough to process now so I completed my tasks and left, rather rapidly, while looking over my shoulder often.

This spirit visited me each time I stayed to process cremains and I became accustomed to it. Each time I heard the door, I would say, "Hey, good evening. How're you doing?" I never got an answer. One evening I said, "Hey, how're you doing? How's life treating you?" Then, I winced at what I'd just said and uttered, "Sorry, dude." This time I received a chuckle in return along with the sniffles.

Only twice did this spirit get close to the area I worked in. He had always gone over to the opposite side of the room as if he were looking for something. But one evening he walked up to the pulverizing processor, which is the machine we use to turn larger pieces into fine ash. I was three feet away from the pulverizer when he did his usual door opening and closing. This particular evening, instead of his footsteps going across the room, they came close to where I stood. I turned around to see a glowing ghostly image of a man walk up to the processor and look down at the opening. He turned toward me, nodded, and walked away, going back out the door.

The second time he got close to me was one evening when I had completed processing and packaging seven sets of cremains. It had been a long day and my shoulders were tight. The tension was giving me a headache. I was engrossed in my work and didn't hear the door open and close. I had my back to the room when I felt a strong pair of hands on my shoulders that gave me a much-needed shoulder massage.

"Oh, that feels good." I said. Then it hit me that no other living person was there except for me, and the massage had to be coming from just one source. I froze while thinking, "How nice, how could this hurt?"

The shoulder massage lasted a minute; I felt a light pat on my right shoulder and felt more than heard, "Better?"

"Yes, thank you," I replied. I heard the footsteps walk away and turned around to see the glowing ghostly image once again. He turned his head in my direction and nodded like before.

Now that I no longer work at Sherwood, I sometimes wonder if my busy, ghostly colleague has anyone to talk with or to check on. He's one of the spirits I miss. I can't say that I would say the same for some others, though.

There is a lot of paperwork involved with a cremation; crematories cannot afford a mistake. At Firewood Hearth Crematory, another place I would sometimes fill in at, I was asked to help out with the paperwork, along with processing and packaging of cremains. Only cremations were done at Firewood. They owned several massive coolers housed inside a large building that also held four retorts, the office, and an employee lounge. Occasionally, I heard banging coming from the largest cooler, which had the capacity to hold up to forty bodies in their cremation containers and was located closest to the retorts and the office. The banging would start at odd times and sometimes go on for twenty to thirty minutes. This unnerved me and gave me the creeps.

One Saturday afternoon, I was assisting with cremations at Firewood when the banging went on and on, but the cremation manager did not seem to notice. He and I were the only people on the property and the sound was very irritating, so I brought it to his attention.

"Yep, I hear it," he said as he prepared to reload one of the retorts.

"Well, what's causing that? It's really annoying. Can we stop it?" I asked.

He gave a nasal-sounding chuckle and said with a rather weary look on his face, "If I could stop it, I would have done it long ago. I wish someone could get it to stop."

"What's causing it?" I nicely asked.

"You really don't want to know." He turned away and proceeded with the reloading. He was done with me and my questions.

The banging stopped and started all afternoon and grated on my last nerve. No matter how engrossed I was in my paperwork or how busy I kept myself, I couldn't tune out the ghoulish din. We'd hear three bangs, then a pause, one or two bangs, then another longer pause, a succession of bangs, and then they would stop for a while, but start up again in a different rhythm. I walked over to the cooler trying to figure out exactly where the sound was coming from.

I figured the banging was coming from *inside* the cooler. As I reached for the door handle, the manager grabbed my hand and pulled me away from the door. He held on tightly to my wrist so I could not slug him.

"No, no, no, no," he vehemently told me. "Don't open that damn cooler when the banging is going on. I warn you!" He was not fooling, and he was also very frightened as his eyes darted from me to the cooler and back to me.

When all the retorts were loaded and in process, and I was caught up on my paperwork, the manager and I took a much-needed break. We grabbed some coffee and sat at one of the picnic benches just outside the main delivery area, overlooking a peaceful, sunny pond in the cemetery next door. When we sat down, he immediately lit up a cigarette; I noticed he was shaking like a leaf.

"I guess you'd like an explanation for my behavior in there," the manager finally said, turning to me. I answered that it would be nice to know what was going on, if he could talk about it.

"A couple of years back," he began, "we had this young guy working here who thought he was invincible. He had some acrobat training that made him think he could climb all over the shelves to position bodies on the top rungs."

I thought about Firewood's cooler with all of its long, steel-mesh shelves that rose twenty feet high. I knew that two people were supposed to work together to position the bodies and bring them in their containers down—one operating the special forklift that carried a securely fastened second person up to the higher shelves. There were many straps on those shelves all used to secure the dead on the higher levels.

"We told him, time and time again, to keep himself off the upper shelves. We didn't know how sturdy they were if they had moving weight on them. He was working here alone one night, doing a lot of the work you're helping us with today, and he must have gotten the hare-brained idea to start lowering bodies for the morning. Something went wrong and he accidentally hung himself by a strap attached to one of the shelves."

The crematory manager lowered his head and I could tell remembering this story was hard on him. I reached across the picnic table and gave him a consoling pat on his hand while letting him know he didn't have to tell me anymore.

"No. I've told you this much so you should know the rest," he said lifting his head. "Then, you'll understand why you can't open that damn cooler door when the banging is going on.

"See," he continued, "the kid must've panicked or something, maybe he was stoned, we don't know. At any time, he could've grabbed the supports for the shelves and just pulled himself up, if he'd wanted to, but he didn't. When we found him the next morning we saw the scuff marks on the wall where he'd kicked at it. The detectives pointed them out to us and asked if anyone else had been with him that evening. None of us had been here. But that's not to say that maybe a friend of his wasn't here or something. His ghost bangs on that wall. We hate it and we've learned to tune it out; just like you'd better learn to do when you're filling in here."

My curiosity was piqued. "Has anyone ever been brought in here to clear the place, get him to calm down and move on? Or does it only happen at certain times?"

"They've been here: priests, psychics, people with tarot cards, counselors. You name it, they've all been here," he answered cynically. "And it still goes on. Whatever that kid is hanging around for, all I can say is that he's mad, damn mad. And he'll attack anyone who opens that damn door when he's doing his thing in there. That's why we pull the bodies in groups. We never know when he's going to start up, and we won't go in there except when we have to. The less that door opens the better.

"Now, this doesn't happen every day; just around the weekends. That's why we try to stay caught up and not have to work over the weekend, like we are today."

An hour or so later, the manager was working in the cooler and I was processing cremains from an earlier run. He pulled the next run of bodies and wheeled number two into the retort area when the banging began again. The manager and I looked at each other, then to the cooler door, which he had left open to go back for body number three. We both took off running to shut that door, but he shoved me out of the way. When he got to the door, a hurricane force wind came out of the cooler along with a voice that yelled "no!" The wind hit the manager and tossed him onto his back causing him to slide a couple feet. I made a move toward him and the cooler but was stopped by a stern glare from the manager along with a running string of expletives.

The manager crawled his way to the cooler door and pushed with all his might. With great force and determination, he shut and bolted the door. The room fell silent.

The manager stood, dusted himself off, straightened his hair and clothing, and walked over to me.

"See what I mean? He's ornery," he said with breathless nonchalance.

"What about the third body?" I asked.

"It can damn well wait," he answered, and he walked off to load the two retorts with the bodies he'd already pulled.

I went on as if nothing had happened. Having gotten the paperwork done, I was informed I'd done a perfect job. The banging didn't start again the rest of that day. I assume the banging is still going on, and the young man is still angry.

When someone decides to become a mortician, they often feel that their responsibility as caretakers to the dead lasts through eternity. Just because an individual may leave the field or retire does not cut them off from their responsibility. It is still in their blood, their soul, and their very existence. As we've seen in other chapters, some of these special morticians, embalmers, and cemeterians will still be at their posts even after death. They will be showing respect and caring for the dead, in their way, throughout eternity, just as we who are living will care for those who are left unclaimed on our shelves.

Almost every funeral home has an area, somewhere in the back of the building, dedicated to the storage of unclaimed cremains. Yes, people leave their loved ones with us, with no further instructions as to where to put them. These storage rooms tend to have odd energies around them.

I was working for Sherwood Mortuary and Cremation Service and had just loaded the van with a body I had removed from a long-term care facility. As I unlocked the driver's door to get into the van and head back to the mortuary, one of the women who worked in the facility flagged me down. Breathlessly, she asked me to do her a favor. She asked me to go to wherever we stored people's ashes and talk to her husband. I was to let him know that she would be in to get him soon. She had been too busy to show up. I let her know I would deliver his cremains to her, at no cost, if that could help her. But she would have nothing to do with that. I promised to convey her message.

I returned to the funeral home, moved the deceased into the cooler after placing fresh identification on the body, and double-checked the accompanying paperwork. After this was done, I proceeded to the cremains storage area. It took me awhile to locate the box containing the cremains of the lady's dearly departed husband as there were no less than forty other individuals on the shelves with him. We also stored them in chronological order, not alphabetical. She had neglected to tell me when her husband had passed. Finally, I found the box containing her husband's cremains and found he had been with us quite some time.

I had never really spent any time in the area before and felt odd when I realized these innocuous boxes held the last cremains of people; and all these people, these boxes, had names. I became depressed and my feet felt as if they were glued to the floor. I tried to move my feet but they would not budge. I began to panic, but instead got the idea to take my feet out of my shoes. Perhaps someone had spilled glue where I was standing. My feet would not come out of my shoes either.

Suddenly, the area got very cold and the lights flickered. I wondered if some sort of spirit energy was here that didn't want me to leave. I decided to talk to it. I let it know that I was there to take care of them, for the time being, not ignore them. I let the energy, if any was there, know that I would return. My feet remained stuck fast to the floor. The room, with its cement floors, brick walls, and no air conditioning, got even colder. I kept speaking to the energy. I felt claustrophobic. I told the energy I had other things to take care of; if I wasn't released, I couldn't take care of them and get them back to their families. That did it.

My feet were free and I could now move them, getting myself away from the area. I went into the office and told one of my co-workers about what had just happened.

"You didn't actually go back there and do what that woman asked, did you?" she asked with a frightened look on her face. I told her that I had.

"You can't do that," she warned with a touch of panic in her tone, "not back there. There's something back there and it gets a hold of you. I won't go back there for anything." She told me not to do anything more for those cremains. I told her I would like to get them back to their families, at least some of them.

"Good luck!" she cried. "Personally, I think there's a reason a lot of them are left here. Some of them, maybe their families just don't care. But I know for a fact that others are left here because they were very unkind to others when they were alive. The families want them out of their lives. That's one of the things we funeral people have to deal with: a person's evil. Bet they didn't teach you that in mortuary school!"

I let the subject drop for several days, but it was brought back to my attention when I was asked to place another unwanted box of cremains in the storage area and grab a fresh package of socks off a shelf in the far end of the long, narrow room for a director who needed to finish dressing someone's feet.

I walked back there with the box of cremains, and thank goodness, the lights were on. I placed the box on a shelf, noticed the one I'd visited before, and took a moment to say a prayer. I went to the back wall to get the socks from the shelf. As I checked the socks to make sure of their color, I turned to leave and felt, more than heard, a low rumble in front of me. I felt sick to my stomach as I looked up.

I saw a nearly solid, dark, smoky cloud swirling and hovering above the floor, blocking my way to the exit. The rumble was coming from the cloud. It was moving toward me slowly, fifteen feet away, but felt much closer. The cloud was backing me up against the shelves. I felt like I couldn't breathe, as if something was pressing on my chest; my distress came from the cloud.

As it moved closer, I felt the sound, and I smelled burning hair with a touch of sulfur. The thought of sulfur did not give me a good mental picture.

The cloud was now five feet from me and I was pressed into the shelving unit, still holding onto the socks. The smell of burning hair and sulfur was overpowering, but I refused to give in to whatever it wanted. The cloud stopped moving toward me and hovered, churning and rumbling. I took this opportunity to move and did a Jackie Chan–type roll on the floor and under the cloud. I got up on my feet, snidely waved good-bye, and took off out of the room.

On my way back to the office, one of the other embalmers walked past me.

He stopped in his tracks and asked amusedly, "What have you gotten into?"

"Why?" I asked.

"It looks like you've been cleaning a fireplace using your body as a rag. You're covered in soot or something," he sniffed in my direction. "You don't smell so good either. Pew!" He turned and walked off. I hadn't noticed my clothes or hands until now. I looked at myself in a mirror near the office entry and saw that I was covered in soot, from head to foot. I did indeed look as if I had been cleaning a fireplace, but thank goodness the socks were in their original plastic and clean.

I walked into the office with socks in hand and handed the pack to the director who had asked for it. He took them, saw my hands and the soot on the outside of the package, then slowly followed my arm up to my face, hair, and clothing. I stood there, disgruntled and embarrassed.

He cracked up and then asked, while totally falling apart with laughter, "What happened? Did you decide to take a roll in the retort? No, I know. A box of cremains blew up on you, didn't it? They get so frisky back there sometimes."

"You went back there again, didn't you?" said the woman I had chatted with days earlier. I nodded and when I did so, black soot fell off my head in a cloud. I blew fresh air upwards in an effort to keep it out of my eyes.

My supervisor came out of his office to see who was laughing and why, but he managed to keep his composure when he saw my condition. He walked up to my purse and keys, picked them up and handed them to me. He told me to go home, take a shower, and he would call me later. I gladly left.

I got home and cleaned up; very grateful that water could get the sooty stuff off, along with the stink.

Several hours later my supervisor called. He asked if I was okay and if I was still mad. When I told him I was, surprisingly, he said, "Good! Remember that feeling the next time you have to go back there. That mad feeling will make it leave you alone. It does that to women; only women!"

I went back to that storage room several days later to put two boxes of cremains on the shelf for storage. Employees who had brought other things into the room had made a mess of the entire area. I knew that clothing had been dropped off for deceased individuals and had never been claimed. It too was supposed to be stored in the cremains storage room, but I saw nothing hanging on the rack. The black, sooty cloud had not appeared so I decided to find the clothing and store it properly.

I located a pile of clothing in the garage, stored on a rack, between two rental caskets. I picked up the pile so I could move it to where it belonged. As I turned around, Ol' Stinky Cloud was ten feet in front of me. It hung in mid-air doing its swirly cloud thing with the low rumble felt and not heard. This time, I was ready.

I moved toward the door, trying not to confront the thing, when it began to move closer to me like before. I cocked my head like I was about to head-butt the thing and set my jaw. I refused to get dirty and stinky again. I glared and fumed like a bull. It moved away and appeared to be taken aback by my actions.

"So, you're nothing but a bully," I strongly stated. "Well, well, well. You stay away from me, Bub." I was able to walk past the cloud without incident.

I moved into the cremains storage area and began hanging clothes on the rack. A sick feeling began to come over me again. I knew that if I turned around I would see Ol' Stinky hanging there. I looked over my shoulder and was right. I decided to ignore it, all the while knowing it was advancing toward me.

I kept my attitude on and forcefully said, "Back off, Stinky. I'm busy." The area got colder, but I didn't let up. "Are you deaf? I said back off!"

"I'm not anywhere near you," a man's voice said, which made me jump. Ol' Stinky had never spoken before. I spun around, almost fell over, and saw my supervisor standing there. The door was open allowing cold air into the room.

"Was it here again?" he asked. "I came to check on you; you were gone too long." I informed him of what had just transpired between me and the cloud. "Okay, good, you're okay. I'll leave you to finish hanging the clothes." He walked out of the room, slamming the door loudly, which stung my ears.

After getting the stinging to stop, I said, "Well, Stinky, at least you don't slam doors," and went back to hanging the clothing.

When I returned to the office, one of the employees let me know he was sorry for not hanging those clothes up earlier. He told me he had been scared off his rear end the last time he'd gone into that area of the garage. He thought he had seen a weird, black cloud come into the room. He wondered if the crematory retorts needed cleaning and was the cause of it.

Later, I did some research on these phenomena and found that the dark, sooty, stinky cloud was actually collective energy from the people who had been abandoned; it is pain with anger that cannot be resolved.

Some of us in the business try to do something positive for these souls by getting a family member to take responsibility for their loved one or we entomb them in a cemetery mausoleum ourselves. If you visit a cemetery's mausoleum and see one crypt with many name plaques on it, that's just one of the ways we legally, morally, ethically and respectfully honor the forgotten ones, the abandoned ones, and act as their caretakers, throughout eternity.

CHAPTER 15

NO SLEEPING TONIGHT!

Sleep is something that disappears from the lives of funeral directors. We mainly lose sleep because we're on call. When the phone rings we never know if it is in regard to someone who has died, someone who is about to die with family or friends shopping around for prices, or someone who just wants to talk. In any case, we're there at all hours of the night when we're needed. Being on call is never fun, but we know that we're needed and that's what we're there for.

I spent many long nights being on call. The worst times were when a call came about a child who had passed, but car wrecks were stressful, too. Often, if I watched the news and saw something tragic, I wondered how long it would take before a call came from the family. I often received phone calls at two in the morning from someone who needed help or just wanted to chat about their loved one whom they'd recently lost.

But whether I was on call in my home or sitting in a general on-call phone room, while doing some crochet to pass the time or reading a book to stay awake, I would often hear or smell something odd before the phone rang. I've heard the sound of car wrecks in my house. I've smelt burnt flesh in a casket room with no crematory on the premises. I've had doorbells ring in the middle of the night with nobody there. Because of those indicators, I knew the phone would ring long before it did.

One night I was sitting in a general on-call area and heard someone wandering around in the empty mortuary portion of the building. I poked my head out of the phone room and into the darkened corridor and heard someone who was very angry in one of the side offices. I heard papers being tossed about and saw lights going on and off. I heard the sounds of casket lids opening and closing while someone repeatedly yelled "no!" I recognized the voice from somewhere and knew this angry individual was some-one who worked there, but I couldn't place the voice. As I was supposed to be the only person in the building, I had to check it out. I grabbed a cell phone and a can of pepper spray and cautiously approached the noisy office.

As I neared the door, the lights went out and the room became silent. I reached around the wall, flicked the lights back on, and peered into the demolished room as papers gently floated down to the desks, chairs, and floor. Silence reigned except for the sound of falling papers, but no one was in the room. Suddenly, the ruckus started up in another room farther down the hall; I ran in to see a similar mess with no one in that room either. Yet again, sounds exploded in another office; I walked in to find papers settling on anything at random and trash strewn all over the floor. I followed the male voice loudly exclaiming "no!" in each room and through each mess. The fray ended as the voice made its way to the back door of the mortuary, which now stood wide open. Nothing had ever happened during other nights I'd been on call in this remote location, but this reeked of spirit activity and I knew something bad had happened.

After the angry disturbance died down, I was attempting to clean up the mess when the on-call phone rang. It was a co-worker who was heading home for the evening. She had passed a terrible wreck on the freeway where the car involved looked just like one that belonged to a director who worked out of the location with the on-call room. She hoped that he was okay, but my heart told me that he wasn't as his face snapped into my mind as being connected with the angry voice of the spirit messing up the offices. Around noon the next day, we received the call we hoped we wouldn't get—he indeed would never return to work again, and we would soon be called to pick up his body from the medical examiner.

Newly deceased individuals tend to make themselves known when one is on call. One night, during a full moon, it was very busy in the phone room. The phones rang frequently and our body removal crews were constantly on the road being dispatched for removals. It was a sad evening for many. Oddly, every time one of our exhausted crews completed a removal and came into the phone room to grab a cup of coffee and put their feet up, either the back doorbell rang or a knock was heard on the glass front door.

This went on from ten p.m. to one a.m. Each time, the crewman who answered the door saw a balding man wearing a hospital gown, robe, and slippers who turned and walked away as soon as the door was touched. By the time the door could be unlocked, the man in the robe would be close to one of the corners of the building. As the crewman approached him, the balding man would turn the corner and disappear.

The guys were quite out of their element on this one. They asked if I was nervous to be alone when they all left on runs. I let them know I was fine, even though I was a touch antsy, but I didn't want them to worry. By this time, I had been around funeral homes for a while and had a good idea of what was going on. I expected a call and it finally came, or in this case, *they* came.

Around three in the morning, while alone in the chilly, cramped phone room, the phone rang. As I answered it, the caller hung up. This happened five more times. When one of the removal teams returned, I asked the two guys if one of them would be so kind as to answer the phone the next time it rang. I felt that whoever was on the other end wanted to speak with a man instead of a woman. I was right.

Sure enough, the phone rang again and the eldest of the two answered the phone while his partner and I watched as he tried to handle the call. The middle-aged driver had seen everything during removals and was well seasoned, but he suddenly became white as a ghost, dropped the phone, and fell to the floor.

After a few minutes he was fine and able to share with us what he'd heard on the phone. He said that the voice on the phone was raspy and asked why we wouldn't let him in. The raspy-voiced man wanted to talk about what he wanted for a funeral, and said he was tired of wandering and didn't like being chased around the building, especially since he had just died.

"I'm kinda tired from all this," he told us the voice had said and asked if we heard the conversation, too. To him, the caller's voice sounded as if it was coming from inside the building, not off-site, and the voice echoed as if it were just in the next room. We had heard nothing out of the ordinary.

His partner and I looked at each other; I could tell he didn't want to believe what his experienced partner was telling us. I had a good idea that the phone would ring again and told them to prepare themselves. They stared at me, silent as the grave, when the phone rang again.

We froze in our positions as we gazed at the ringing phone. I nodded for one of them to answer; the younger partner decided to listen in as the elder answered. After listening to the raspy voice on the phone and telling the voice "Soon, sir," the elder crewman hung up in shock.

"How did you know we'd get a repeat call like that? How did you know and what's going on here?" he shakily asked me.

"It's like this," I told them. "There's an older gentleman who has died, probably in a hospital since he's wearing a hospital gown. He probably passed around ten and we're going to get a call, hopefully soon, to pick him up. It's that simple."

"Okay, that's all fine and good, but how do you know?" the insistent driver asked. This was tough to explain, so I decided the truth would be best.

"I'm a bit sensitive to the energy of spirits, er, ghosts. The man who has been coming up to the door and disappearing when you get close is one of them." At this point their jaws all dropped.

Just after three, a call came in from a nurse at a nearby hospital. She asked that we pick up a gentleman who had passed earlier that evening. The crews, who had come back in from their runs, drew straws to see which would go out on this call; they were a little spooked. The crew who drew the short straw was the same crew that had answered the phone earlier.

When they returned and had placed the gentleman in the cooler, they entered the phone room. They sat on the couch on the opposite side of the room.

"It was him, the guy, the old guy. You know, him," the elder crewman said as his younger partner nodded.

"The gentleman at the door in the hospital gown?" I asked.

"Yes, him," he replied. "He died about half past ten and his family didn't want us to come for him until they'd left around three. His nurse told us that his family felt really bad; the old guy wanted to take one last walk and didn't get to. He really liked to walk."

Obviously, the old gentleman did take his last walk. Me? I was never asked to be on-call at that phone room again.

Many years ago, the mortician and his family lived in the mortuary. When a family required the services of the mortician, the body was taken to his home. All the preparations were completed with the viewing taking place in the parlor or living room. The casketed body was then taken to a service in a church, followed by the final rest at a cemetery. That's why a mortuary is still called a funeral home. Most funeral homes do not have the family living on the premises today. However, to many of us a funeral home can be a home away from home.

Some of us find the peace and serenity of the mortuary more hospitable than staying home if we've had a difficult evening with our spouse or if the power has gone out. There are also times when a living person must stay in the funeral home overnight to see to the needs of the dead. I was one of the few individuals who would willingly perform this all-night watch. Usually, I took a sleeping bag and camped out on a couch or the floor of a chapel.

One night, I stayed all night at Serenity Shores due to the fact that someone had been murdered in the parking lot during a visitation. I had spoken to the victim earlier in the evening just as he was leaving after attending a viewing and just prior to him being killed by someone who must have been out near his car. The police officers didn't give me the okay to leave until three in the morning, so I thought I'd lock up and babysit the building all night. After all, the funeral home had become like a second home to me and I felt like someone had died on my property.

I was the only living body in the mortuary after the viewing's visitors were finally permitted to leave. The police and detectives were out in the parking lot conferring among themselves. As I went about my business inside the funeral home, I glanced out a window and saw the deceased victim wandering aimlessly around the parking lot.

I had heard of spirits hanging around an area after being murdered or killed in a car wreck, but had never experienced it firsthand. I kept my eye on the young man's spirit through the window. He approached many different people working the scene, but did not get a response from them. I could see him, but did not know if I could hear him and thought I would give it a shot to try to help him.

I snuck out a side door and made my way to the parking lot, trying to make myself inconspicuous among the throng of police vehicles. As I neared the spirit, an older woman approached him. She had appeared out of nowhere wearing a floral apron over a house dress styled from the sixties. He acted as if he knew her. When he saw her, he stopped and covered his mouth. As she got closer to him with her hand out, he sank to his knees and began to sob into his open palms.

Even though I was more than ten yards away from the spirits, I heard him sobbing over the noise of the officials and the radios in their vehicles. I looked around at the officers concentrating on their investigation and none of them acknowledged what was happening right in front of them.

The woman lightly touched the man on his bowed head. My heart ached for this man who was so newly dead. The woman took him by the hand. They walked off together in the direction she had come from and disappeared. But just before disappearing, the two paused and turned in my direction. They focused on me and the man raised his right hand and gave me a wave. I gave him a nod and was relieved that someone loved him enough to come back across from the other side to safely escort him home.

Celebrity or high-profile funerals can be unpredictable events. People who are obsessed with celebrities of any kind will do anything to get at the deceased. Some will even attempt to steal the body. That's why someone is often needed twenty-four hours a day to stay with a body until it is laid in the ground or sealed in a tomb.

One evening at Serenity Shores we were on special high alert. We had the body of a much decorated young military man in his casket, ready to go to the cemetery the next morning. We had already moved him twice to keep media, the public, and protestors away and off-guard. The second funeral home we had located him in was broken into by people who were in strict opposition to the ongoing war. They showed no respect for the fact that this was now someone's dead son, not a piece of government property.

We had brought him back to our location and hid him. Since I lived close by and have insomnia, I volunteered to stay the night.

I set up camp in the kitchen. From there, I could hear everything, but someone up to no good couldn't hear or see me. All was quiet and calm until about two in the morning. At that time, I distinctly heard battlefield sounds off in the distance. I heard troops marching. The sounds of men laughing and talking as if in a mess hall came from somewhere, but nowhere.

I walked around the inside of the building, being careful not to turn on any lights that could be seen from the outside. As I went from room to room, chapel to parlor, I still heard the sounds. Out in the parking lot there wasn't a soul, none that I could see anyway. That changed at 0300 hours.

I looked out the front windows of the funeral home to check the parking lot again. Gazing out into the night, I saw a thick cloud of fog move along the black asphalt driveway. It was a cold night and had rained earlier so I thought nothing of it, until the cloud began to change.

The fog began to glow a heavenly blue and out of it, from the right and from the left, came two beautifully tall and proud military men fully armed for guard duty wearing full-dress uniforms. They were the same branch of the military as my young charge and positioned themselves on either side of the front doors of the funeral home. These ethereal centurions faced out toward the public parking area. They were perfect in every way, even down to the spit-shined, black shoes on their feet that never touched the ground. I found that the young man's comrades-in-arms positioned themselves at each and every entrance to the building; he and I were completely safe.

After my young charge's spirit guard went on duty, the sounds diminished as night turned into day. The battle-field sounds ceased and the marching slowed to the same cadence done by the casket honor guard at cemeteries. I thought to myself, "They're coming to take their fallen brother home." It was apparent they knew he was in the building.

At the break of dawn, I heard the spirit-like sound of a bugle playing "Taps" in the distance. As rays of sunlight broke through the clouds and in the front windows of the lobby, they illuminated a table that contained a framed photo of the young man. I wiped the tears from my eyes that always appear when I hear "Taps," and knowing this would be a special day, proceeded to get my young charge ready for his final escort home.

To all of you,
Whose Day Is Done,
Your spirits soar
With each new sun.

I remove my hat,
To you raise a glass,
And pray to Heaven,
No more must pass.

CHAPTER 16

SOME FUN DURING
THE FINAL RIDE

The Final Ride is the term for the last journey someone takes after they die, whether by hearse, van, truck, or cremains sent through the U.S. Postal Service. We initially pick up the dead from hospitals, hospice facilities, private homes, the medical examiners' office, and even other mortuaries. We then deliver them to a mortuary or a central care facility where they're prepared for their final journey. During the drive to the cemetery, crematory, or church—their final ride—things can get interesting.

When we roll a casket into the back of the coach, we use a padded, steel bumper with a steel pin on the bottom of it that anchors into a row of holes in a steel frame in the bed of the coach. This bumper has a screw-like hand crank that allows us to adjust the bumper to fit the length of the casket and hold it securely in place. When not in use, this bumper is stored in a compartment over the fender.

Prior to embarking on the final ride for a dear woman who loved to shop, my assistant and I loaded her casket into the hearse and secured it with the bumper. We knew we would be in for a bumpy ride as her last request was to have her procession drive slowly past the front door of her favorite superstore, which would also take us over some speed bumps. With all permissions attained from the store manager, the escorts at attention, and the cemetery waiting, we rolled out.

Proceeding toward her final destination, we entered the store parking lot being careful not to bottom out the hearse. As we rolled slowly over the last of the speed bumps, immediately in front of the door to the store, her casket gave a lurch. We signaled to the escort leader that we needed to stop to check on the casket. We were right in front of the store's glass doors and viewable to all patrons, but we had no choice. The manager was standing there out of respect for one of his most frequent shoppers, and I let him know what we had to do.

I ran to the back of the hearse and opened the door. The casket had not only lurched but shifted to an angle. Thinking the bumper had become dislodged while going over the bumps, I looked for it; it was nowhere to be found. I began to panic as we were holding up the line and regular traffic began to back up behind us. Something told me to look in the storage compartment for the bumper. When I did, I found it secured in its case as if it had never been taken out.

I realigned the casket, thanking the heavens the woman was light, and re-secured the casket with the bumper. While making my way back into the hearse, the manager yelled out, "Hey, we've got some great sales on some of her favorite things right now; maybe she just wants to go shopping."

We proceeded to the cemetery without incident. During the sermon portion of her graveside service, her pastor added, "I'm sure our dear sister is racing in to that big blue-light special in the sky; she almost went into the store during her final ride. Oh, Sister did so love to shop. May her heavenly debit card never be overdrawn. Amen."

Spirits can often change radio stations when they're in a room. This also applies to when they are taking their final ride. On one ride, we had a problem with the hearse's stereo while on a long, eighty-mile drive out of town with a loaded casket in the back. My assistant, Jim, and I tried several CDs, tapes, and the radio, but nothing would play.

As I was driving the hearse, Jim worked on adjusting the radio and found a station playing a tune by ZZ Top, a famous band out of the great state of Texas that knows how to rock. Jim and I didn't mind at all, but absolutely no other channel came in clearly for us. While we listened to the opening rifts of "Sharp Dressed Man" the radio volume cranked full blast. We looked at each other questioningly, knowing neither of us had touched the controls. We tried to turn down the volume, but it turned itself back up.

We decided to leave the volume alone just in case this was a final request from our guest in the back. At the end of the song, the station began playing a tune by another artist; the radio went dead and turned off on its own.

"I wonder..." Jim said and dug into the tape box we had hidden between the black leather seats. He pulled out a tape of ZZ Top's greatest hits and asked if he should give it a try.

"Give it a shot," I said. "This is *his* ride. He seems to be the one calling the shots here."

Jim popped in the tape and it immediately turned on. The volume once again cranked up seemingly by itself, and we rocked on to the cemetery with our own sharp dressed man.

Radios, tape decks, and CD players; spirits will turn on these electronics when one least expects it. We often heard music playing in the hearse at all hours of the day and night—without the keys in the ignition. We have also found that the hearse lights would go on and off as we drove by certain destinations such as churches, schools, or arenas. Spirits do like to play.

I have experienced times when the casket lid opens while en route. Fortunately, the lid can't raise very high, as the vehicle roof is only eight to ten inches above the casket's lid, but this can become a problem.

While on yet another out-of-town trek to a cemetery we had never been to before, Jim and I stopped at a convenience store in the town to ask for directions to the cemetery. While Jim went inside, I got out, locked up the hearse, and took in the beautiful scenery while stretching my legs. As I breathed in the crisp, clean air of the mountainous region, I heard a scream behind me.

I quickly turned to see a woman peering into the side window of the hearse and pointing. I ran to her side and she said that she'd seen the casket lid raise and lower. I calmed her and told her that sometimes casket lids will raise and lower due to pressure and altitude changes on a long drive. This malarkey seemed to satisfy her and she headed off toward the bar next door.

I climbed back into the hearse, reached through the dividing window, and found that I could indeed lift the casket's lid; something seemed to be blocking the lid from closing all the way. This concerned me as I had shut and locked the lid myself prior to loading. There was no way I could pull the casket out now, in this location, and check to see what was the matter.

Jim arrived back at the hearse with a bag full of snacks and a couple cans of pop. We sat in the hearse and enjoyed our high-caloric, low-nutrition treat that tasted oh, so good after a two-hour drive, and I filled him in on what had happened while he was in the store.

"We always have spirit adventures, don't we?" he laughed. I agreed as I started up the coach.

We arrived at the small cemetery in the hills and looked for the sextant who was also the local mortician; neither of us could locate him. We decided to take the casket out of the hearse, place it onto the rolling cemetery cot, and give it a good once over. When we had the casket carefully centered on the cot, we examined the lid. Sure enough, not only was the casket unlocked, it was open about the thickness of a pencil and the lid wouldn't close.

When the cemetery mortician found us, we explained the situation about the open casket and he threw his head back and let out a huge belly laugh.

"That happens up here all the time," he said. "Go ahead and open her casket for a minute. We're used to it up here. They really love the view and just want to see it one more time. Go ahead."

So we opened up the casket and gave her some private time with nature. When we saw her family arriving at the cemetery, we closed and locked the lid for the last time. The rest of her service went off without a hitch. It was a good day.

Whichever name one prefers to call it, either coach or hearse, there always seems to be an air of mystery with a little magic surrounding this final transport vehicle. This big, beautiful, sturdy car has been known to bring two opposing forces together.

One evening while working at Serenity Shores, I had the honor of being in charge of a visitation that took the deceased and me to a house of worship instead of staying in the mortuary's chapel. The church was airy, light, and refreshing with a positive feeling to it, but was located in a very depressed area of town.

Prior to leaving with the deceased, one of the funeral directors who had been to the church before told me to keep an eye out for any criminal activity.

"Don't let that coach out of your sight!" he told me with a finger-wag in my face. I had no intention of letting anyone harm the one-hundred-thousand-dollar hearse and didn't much appreciate the finger-wag, but thanked him for the advice anyway.

I arrived on the scene, but my assistant for the evening was nowhere to be found. I waited for a bit to begin unloading, hoping she would meet me there as she had been instructed to. She didn't, so I went to find some assistance in the church. I located one of the ministers in the pastor's lounge and hated asking for help, but had no alternative. He let me know he'd just had back surgery and could help by unlocking the church but that was all. That was okay; I could do it alone, but it would take longer.

He followed me to the hearse and felt I would definitely need some help when he saw the large casket. He put his fingers to his mouth and gave a whistle that pierced the air, causing my ears to ring. As the ringing cleared, two defiant-looking boys walked around the corner of the building and stopped on either side of the minister.

These two young teenagers looked as if they'd been through a war. They didn't seem comfortable around each other either, as they glared back and forth. I saw that their eyes had seen far too much pain. Sorrow, mistrust, and anger emanated from their very souls. I felt their inner rage and saw the heavy chips on their shoulders necessary for survival. The tattoos on their forearms only drew attention to the scars upon their hands from far too many brutal altercations.

After the minister introduced us, I led the boys to the hearse. Their cocky demeanors changed to aloof boredom when the minister told them they were to give me a hand. But when they got an eyeful of my big, gorgeous, shiny, white Cadillac hearse, their heads came up and so did their posture. These two young, tortured souls smiled joyous smiles of youth. Light came into their eyes as they looked at each other and spoke to each other with shared words of amazement. They walked around the hearse, pointing to different things. They touched each other kindly bringing the other's attention to something on the car the other hadn't seen. They laughed, they talked, and they were young as they should be, all because of a hearse.

The minister and I quietly observed this delightful display. I found myself smiling at the exuberance and amazement of youth; then, I looked at the minister standing next to me with his arms folded and one hand going up to his cheek to wipe away a tear.

The attitudes of the boys changed for the better, and they were the best assistants I could have asked for. Even though they hadn't known the deceased in life, they'd heard she was a good person. They helped me with positioning the flowers I had brought with me near the front of the church and placed the printed material in the lobby for the visitors.

I began to pull the casket onto the church cot, which I can do alone, but the boys politely asked if they could help. I let my young helpers assist and showed them exactly what to do. I expressed the importance of doing this just right and why; they hung on every word.

Although I did most of the work, those two boys, those two young men, worked together and every move they made was precise, attentive, and done with care, honor, and respect; not only for the deceased, but for each other.

During the visitation, with hundreds of people in and out of the church, the boys took it upon themselves to babysit the coach for the entire evening. It had two personal body guards who did their job so extremely well I felt they deserved a treat. So, while they were telling some friends about the hearse, I hit the light switch on the ignition key that I held in my pocket. This made them jump, but they were in awe when they saw the back door open on its own.

After the service, the minister approached me and asked how I had gotten those boys to stop warring with each other and work together. I let him know I had nothing to do with their remarkable metamorphosis. The credit belonged to the hearse.

One of the most inspiring yet amusing hearse stunts we occasionally have the honor to perform is that of a mock funeral procession. The first time I shared in one of these events was at Serenity Shores, and I hadn't been there long. Things never ceased to amaze me back then, and I often found myself giggling over the simplest of things.

One of our families had decided upon cremation for the final disposition of their loved one, yet they still wished to go through the motions of a regular funeral, including seeing the casket in a hearse. My funeral director for the evening told me that we were to act as if we were going to the cemetery after the service.

"At night?" I chimed in.

"Yup!" the funeral director answered. "I'm going to drive off like I'm headed to the cemetery. Then, about twenty minutes later, I'll be back. Just make sure everybody is gone by then. Then we'll be done for the evening."

The service went beautifully. We stoically placed the casket into the hearse, and he drove off with a full casket along for the ride; the final ride that the family needed to see, beautiful and meaningful.

The family promptly left the funeral home, and I cleaned the chapel and waited for his return. Thirty minutes passed, then forty-five and he still hadn't shown up. I dumped all the trash and heard what sounded like someone whispering through the microphone of the tiny chapel—at the time I did not know what this was and wanted to leave. But an hour passed and still no hearse.

I had the entire building shut down for the night and did not feel like hanging around in the chapel, so I waited by the open back door. Finally, I saw headlights enter the parking lot.

The director backed up the hearse to the unloading door next to the garage and got out of the car. He began pacing while ranting and waving his arms. He was mad and I didn't know why.

He stopped in mid-stride, looked to the heavens, and lit a cigarette. After a couple of drags, he told me he had decided to make a quick side trip through a drive-thru restaurant to get dinner to take home to his wife. When he realized that it was going to take a long time in line, he knew he couldn't maneuver the hearse out of the line and had to sit there. He was incredibly embarrassed and felt absolutely horrible.

After he finished blowing off some steam, we unloaded the hearse and put it away for the night. The deceased was now safely tucked away and awaiting yet another final ride in the morning to the crematory. All was good.

The final thing he said to me that evening, with bags of hot food in hand, was, "Don't you ever let my wife know her dinner ever sat in a hearse, especially not one with someone in the back. Okay?" No problem, I'll never tell.

CHAPTER 17

CEMETERY ARDOR

I often like to just walk and think. I like to watch birds as they fly and listen to them sing, smell the scent of freshly mown grass, and stop to smell the roses. I also like being somewhere that has all of this, with a touch of history and interesting artwork included. I walk in cemeteries. I love the quiet and serenity along with the sense of safety that these most hallowed grounds offer. Sometimes I'll walk during the day, but I have been known to walk at night when things are quiet and the living are banned. When I'm there, I know I'm never really alone.

I don't encourage nor do I advocate others doing this, as cemeteries are private properties for the most part. They are also hallowed ground and the eternal home to those who reside there; I only do this at night when I'm allowed to. I know my way around and what to look for. I never trespass, for the grounds truly are someone's eternal home.

When one walks respectfully in a cemetery, one usually will come upon unique, unexpected things. Anything from memorial kiosks that provide locations of deceased individuals and their biography, to everlasting lights that illuminate a grave, to interactive tombstones. A cemetery is never boring, especially when the residents come out to play.

While walking in cemeteries, particularly on chilly evenings when the air is crisp and clear, I have been in quiet thought when I've heard the howling of a wolf, the caw of a raven, or the coo of a dove. I have asked office staff if the area was home to interactive tombstones that would produce these sounds and am only given polite negatives in return. Many cemeterians care enough to protect the information of their residents, even from a colleague. So in those instances, I never really know whether I have passed a technological marvel or if spirits have spoken. That doesn't explain open areas where animals are heard, though.

While walking in a cemetery's outlying and undeveloped areas, I have heard animals. One evening, just at sunset, I was walking in an area of undeveloped land connected to a neighboring cemetery. This land was designated for expansion at a later date. I heard a wolf-like howl in the distance, close to the developed and occupied portion of the cemetery behind me. I turned and looked around to figure out where the sound came from.

I suddenly picked up the sound of a very large animal running in my direction. I could hear it breathing as it ran. Low growls were heard advancing with the fall of each step. I turned in all directions looking for the animal, which I felt to be a large hound, and saw nothing, but the heavy sound of its feet hitting the dry ground kept coming closer.

I had the sudden urge to cover my head and duck down low to the ground. Off to my right, the sound of the animal breathing and paws hitting the ground was almost upon me, so down I went.

I heard the animal jump as if to leap over something, follwed by a moment of silence, then the sound of it landing on the dry ground to my left. The sound of breathing and running paws continued. I followed the sound with my eyes as it faded away. I took a few steps in the direction of the sound's movement and looked down at my feet. There, in the dry, dusty earth about ten feet away from where I had ducked, were the large tracks of a dog. I retraced my steps and found identical tracks coming from the other direction that ended just feet from where I had ducked.

"A phantom dog," I muttered to myself, "a big phantom dog. I have got to remember that." My walk that evening was over. For some reason, I neglected to notice the sunset.

When a person feels a desire or need to walk in a particular cemetery, graveyard, crypt, or mausoleum's area, they shouldn't be surprised to find that the reason the particular area is brought to their attention may be because someone wishes to be visited.

I have often been in cemeteries while performing my duties of laying someone to their final rest when I have felt as if my foot or pant leg is stuck on something. I have felt tugs on the hem of my pants or felt as if my foot was under a rock and could not move. When I looked to find the problem, what I invariably found was the headstone of someone I had known in life. Quite the flood of emotion took hold at those times, but I kept my composure.

I've returned to visit the old friend that I lost contact with in life, now knowing where to find them.

For those of us who have business in cemeteries, we find that spirits confront us in many ways. The episodes can run the gamut from spectral sightings of people that suddenly disappear, to icy cold hands going up the leg of a bagpiper in a kilt; sounds of animals that are nowhere around or lone crying in the night. We know the difference between ghostly manifestations and perfectly natural phenomena such as that of ignis fatuus.

This is a phenomenon that people often find in photos they have taken in a cemetery or anywhere leaves, brush, animals, and insects may be decaying. *Ignis fatuus* is Medieval Latin for *foolish fire*. It also goes by the name of cemetery lights and corpse candles, among others. When caught on film or seen with the naked eye, particularly at night, it is indeed an impressive sight and worth taking note of. But it's not paranormal in any way.

Ignis fatuus is merely the natural combination of gases produced during the decomposition and putrefaction of anything carbon based. These gases, when exposed to oxygen in the right combination, can spontaneously combust, which is the cause for tiny flames of reddish-gold to bluish-green that are sometimes seen near the ground in cemeteries and floating in darkened areas of swampland and other moist areas. During the day, these small flames may not be seen but smelt instead, similar to the odors of decomposition, rotten eggs, or even flatulence. This is completely natural with a scientific explanation. But this doesn't explain something else that can be caught on photos or with the naked eye.

Many times I have noticed an anomaly that seems to come out of the ground in cemeteries. I have seen what looks like a cloud of rust-colored gas rise out of the soil. The rust color has a slight glow to it that can strengthen or weaken. The glow shifts in intensity depending upon the mood and intention of the living person it presents itself to. I've never been frightened by this phenomenon and have felt no negativity coming from it; neither have others who have experienced this. Often, the cloud moves toward someone who is distraught or sad, enveloping the person as if in a consoling hug. Within just a few minutes, the person is relieved of their angst and can continue on.

This is a very moving experience when it happens, but it seems to take its toll on the rust-colored entity. After the encounter, the color will change from the glowing rust to a muted pink or yellow tone, and it will return to the ground. What this kind and benevolent specter is no one knows for sure. But apparently it's not shy about giving its energy to assist others who require some care and an emotional lift.

Since a cemetery is a deceased person's forever home, if they choose to remain in the area they will often do things there just as they did in their own homes or neighborhoods; even run people off who aren't wanted.

One very dark evening, I had the urge to walk in a cemetery where I'd laid several people to rest. I felt as if I were being called to pay them a visit. I didn't take any cards, flowers, or gifts; just myself and my husband who came along for the ride.

I drove up to the cemetery gates expecting to see them closed and locked, but instead found them wide open. I pulled into the grounds and drove past the office with its lights still on and cars still out front. Knowing that they would have seen me enter, I proceeded onto my first destination, which was the grave of a small child I had laid to rest whose young life had ended tragically. When I located her headstone, I was saddened to find the corpse of a dead baby bird lying upon it. The double loss of innocence moved me to bury the little bird and clean the headstone. I spent some quiet time at the now double grave and moved on.

The next site was of an older woman who had passed of natural causes and was meticulously clean in life. When I located her tombstone, I found it defiled by human excrement. Her location was near some tall bushes that blocked the view of the maintenance crews, so I went to my car and grabbed some latex gloves and paper toweling. After cleaning the mess, I took a few moments to pay my respects.

My husband and I decided to sit for a few minutes on a meditation bench located near the woman's grave. The night stars were lovely, and from our vantage point we could see the lights of the office should they turn off and the employees begin looking for us so that they could lock up. As we sat viewing the night sky, we noticed a car driving slowly through the winding pathways. The vehicle had no lights on, but the light from the waning full moon sparkled on the classic chrome bumpers and tailfins. The way it was moving didn't give any indication whether or not it was that of an employee or someone up to no good, so we exercised caution if it were the latter and moved on to my last stop.

After parking my car one last time in the quietly dark cemetery, I approached my last grave; that of a middle-aged man who had sworn off booze several years before a drunk driver took his life. Off in the distance, in the farthest end of this eastern section of the cemetery, I saw a couple walking away from us and toward the oleander hedges in the distance. I made my way to the sober man's grave and found on his granite monolith a pair of lace panties, several empty beer cans, and a used condom. I ranted viciously during my clean up of the disgusting mess and was appalled at the lack of dignity that some fools show to the dead; apparently I wasn't the only one upset.

Out of nowhere the vehicle my husband and I had seen earlier appeared on the winding pathway my car was parked upon. Instead of it traveling slowly as before, it now barreled in our direction. The car flew past us with lightning speed and seemed to glow. The sound of tires and revving engine came from the vehicle. We saw that the tires didn't touch the ground and flames shot in rooster tails off of them. The headlights came on like lighthouse beacons as the car rose over the monuments and tombstones, aiming for the couple walking toward the oleanders. The brightness of the lights and the rev of the engine alerted the couple to the oncoming threat; they frantically ran off the property, through the bushes, and over a five-foot chain-link fence.

During this chase, my husband and I stood awestruck. After the couple left the grounds, the ethereal car paused in the air near the point where the couple left and moved back and forth as if making sure this highly disrespectful duo had vacated the grounds. The guardian vehicle turned in mid-air and made its way back over the monuments and tombstones that it had crossed over previously and came to rest on the winding roadway. At this point the lights went out and the flames of the tires ceased. It again moved slowly along the winding road and headed straight for where we stood.

My husband had gotten into the passenger side of my car and I was just beginning to, my curiosity piqued at the sight of this spectral phantom, when it pulled alongside our car. We couldn't see the driver or the passenger, nor could we see into the darkness of the interior, but as it passed, a black leather jacketed arm and gloved hand stuck out of the passenger window and gave us both the thumbs-up. We watched the phantom car unceremoniously proceed down the winding road and then quietly disappear.

"I think we just got the thumbs-up from some of your peeps," my husband uttered.

In awe of what had just happened, I replied, "Welcome to my world."

In this cemetery, there is a vintage car buried with its embalmed owner sitting at the wheel. Apparently, he still loves to drive. Don't ask me where it is; I'll never tell.

CHAPTER 18

THEY OFTEN HAVE THE LAST WORD

During my career in the funeral industry I had the honor of being the director or attendant for many people who were well-loved and respected. Many of those services were uneventful and quite moving. One evening while working at Blue Willows Mortuary, however, I was the attendant for the visitation of an elderly woman who turned out to be quite a handful. I hadn't made the arrangements with the family so I didn't know much about her, but she had a stately appearance as she rested peacefully in her casket. The family's funeral director, Marie, said that the woman had been very meticulous in life. The family insisted that everything in the chapel be precisely as the woman had planned before she died.

Prior to leaving the funeral home for the evening, Marie was nervous and twitchy as she repeatedly checked every detail. She checked the music playing on the CD player, the floral arrangements standing at the head and foot of the casket, and the floral spray draped over the foot of the casket. She realigned the memorial folders on the sideboard table near the back entry door that were to be handed to the mourners as they walked in. She adjusted the position of the guest book that sat on an antique, angled-top, raised stand, which held a small light over the pens making it easier for the guests to see to sign it. She checked lighting in the chapel along with the lit candles at the head and foot of the casket many times; everything had to be *just right* she kept muttering to herself as she moved through the building.

I lost count of how many times she approached the casket and fidgeted with the deceased's hair, the fabric of her dress, the folds of the throw on the casket, and the lay of the woman's meticulously manicured hands.

"It's all gotta be just so" she kept repeating under her breath.

Marie was usually confident and calm in her demeanor, so this behavior was not normal in any way. For some reason, this service had her frazzled.

While Marie checked the wick and flame of the candle at the foot of the casket one more time, I asked her if the family had been particularly difficult.

"You might say that," she answered as she wrinkled her mouth and kept glancing toward the occupant of the casket. Jokingly, I asked if the deceased had been acting up. Marie turned ashen and looked at me sternly.

"Do you pray?" she asked as she grabbed hold of my jacket and pulled me into the aisle of the chapel, away from the casket. The combination of her reaction and behavior made me uncomfortable.

"Sure I do. Why?" I cautiously replied.

"Then, I'd do a lot of it tonight, if I were you," she whispered, glancing at the casket. "If you have a rosary in your purse, it wouldn't be a bad idea to keep it on you tonight, too. And, don't forget, please, please, please don't forget to check the flower room doors repeatedly, both the inner door and the outer door. Make double sure they're closed and locked. Please, promise me you'll do that. Please!"

Shakily I replied, "Sure, sure, I promise. What the heck is going on?" I was concerned. The funeral home had been broken into several times; bodies had been defiled, articles had been stolen, graffiti had been sprayed on caskets, and the hearse had been vandalized. I wondered if something along those lines had happened again, or if the neighborhood police had alerted her to a threat to the mortuary.

Her only response, which came out shaky, fearful, and chilling was, "Some people don't like to be dead, my dear." She tightened her grip on my jacket and pulled me toward the chapel entry. "Keep a close eye on that darn flower room door. Check those doors before the last of her group leaves and go out with them; don't be here by yourself. You don't even need to vacuum, they're very tidy people." She never missed a beat while walking backward, pulling me along, and keeping her eyes aimed at the casket behind me.

As we entered the lobby just outside the chapel entrance, she calmed greatly and started with her usual mother-hen behavior that I was so accustomed to. As Marie straightened my lapel and collar and picked pet fur off my jacket, she calmly said, "Now, I'd like you to please keep the music that's on the player playing until the service starts, then turn it off. Start it up again when the service concludes and, as the last of the family leaves, ask them to wait a moment so that you can leave with them. Don't be here by yourself tonight.

"Deacon Tom will be here to recite the rosary prayers for her from seven to eight and they definitely plan to stay until nine. Just leave the CD in the player, leave everything like I have it, and I'll pack it all up in the morning before I take her to the church. I'll wait here for the family to arrive and I'll introduce you; then, I'm going to get the hell out of here!" She said the last three words very emphatically with clenched teeth while looking toward the casket as if angry with someone.

The music played as the family arrived and parked their cars in the lot. Marie walked into the parking lot to greet the family. At this point, I thought it would be a good idea to begin my habit for the evening of checking the flower room doors. As I walked into the chapel and down the aisle toward the casket, I heard a sound of either a moan or the word "no." I thought my ears were playing tricks on me because of Marie's behavior. Having stopped in my tracks when I heard the sound as I walked around the head of the casket and the stands of flowers there, I decided to shake it off and check the flower room. The inner door was locked tight, but I found the outer door leading to the parking lot open about an inch. No more flowers had been delivered for the woman so I closed and locked both doors, securely checked the latches, turned out the light, and left the room.

Across the tiny hallway from the flower room and on the back side of the wall behind the casket, I heard someone moving brass flower stands and a few random notes of organ music in the storage room. I thought Marie had gone in the storage area for a flower stand and had leaned on the organ, so I went in to help. The room was dark and I saw no one when I turned on the lights. Just for the heck of it, I checked the organ and found that it wasn't plugged in; I must have been hearing things. I giggled at myself, shook it off, turned off the light, and left that room. As I walked by the flower room again, the inner door I had just locked and latched was now open.

Slamming the inner door this time, I was confident that this wouldn't happen again. As I walked down the aisle away from the casket, I heard the organ once more. Defiantly, I put my hands on my hips, turned in the direction of the casket, looked about the room, and said, "All right, now you just stop that. It isn't funny. Besides, I have work to do." I turned and went into the lobby where Marie stood with the family and introduced me to them.

After we took the family in the chapel and left them with their loved one for some private alone time, Marie and I went into the office where I let her know that I had locked the doors in the flower room and turned off the lights. She became pale and stared at the floor.

"You locked the doors and turned off the lights?" she calmly asked. When I said I had, she picked up her keys and her purse, and asked me to put my rosary and cell phone in my pocket. As she stepped across the threshold onto the back stoop leading to the parking lot, she turned and looked me straight in the eye.

"I locked those doors and turned out those lights just before you got here," she said and left.

This took place from half past three to four. The family was to have private time alone with their loved one from four to five with the public's visitation from five to seven. The rosary and prayers were to be from seven to eight, with our final exit at nine. No problem and nothing unusual there. I expected Deacon Tom to arrive his usual thirty minutes early for his restful cup of pre-rosary coffee and fun conversation.

I had everything working smooth as silk. The music played, the microphone was ready, the lighting was just right, and the candles in their tall stands flickered beautifully without a spark or splatter. People complimented the coffee and cookies Marie and I had set out. The plumbing, which was old and often noisy, cooperated and kept quiet. I'd checked the flower room doors several times and they remained closed and locked. No funny business out of the little room behind the casket either. All was right with the world and all systems go. Little did I know things were about to change.

Deacon Tom's usual arrival time of half past six came and went. At a quarter to seven, I called his cell number. The good deacon let me know he was having car trouble and would be there by a quarter past seven, at the latest. I told him that I would let the family know.

I walked into the chapel and down the aisle toward the casket and the family seated in the front pew. Bending down in front of the family, I quietly informed them of the deacon's problem. They understood and were nice about the whole thing, but they told me their mother wouldn't understand and that she was already upset. I asked them to point me in Mom's direction and I would explain it to her and calm any fears she may have. They all, at the same time, looked up and pointed toward the casket.

I slowly turned in the direction of their outstretched hands hoping to see a matronly woman standing in front of the casket. Nope, they were indeed referring to the woman *in* the casket.

The deceased woman's son then said, "Did you say Deacon Tom is coming? Why not Father William? Mom's not going to like that! She specifically asked for Father William." I couldn't answer why Father William wasn't coming. They nicely told me to go about my business doing whatever it was that I did and they would talk with mom.

I left the chapel area and saw them cautiously walk up to the casket to talk to mom. They spoke with her for a good ten minutes. I had no idea what they said, but they looked as if they were pleading with her, even apologizing to her. At one point, they looked like they were being chastised by this woman who was so cold and so still.

The door that led from the lobby out to the parking lot suddenly and violently slammed shut. Standing in the lobby near the door, this startled me and caused me to jump. It also made no sense as a forty-pound flowerpot had been holding that door open so that folks could go in and out freely. It was also nice to have some fresh air in the building since it was such a lovely spring evening.

A little after seven, my cell phone rang. It was Marie wondering if everything was going as planned. I let her know that things weren't as we'd hoped, informed her of what was going on, and I heard her fumble with the phone in an effort not to drop it. When she spoke again, she let me know she was enjoying a glass of wine and that it had taken several refills to give her enough courage to call. She was *not* coming back to the mortuary to smooth things over. She began crying and begged me to hold down the fort on my own. I promised her I would; if there were any major problems, then, and only then, would I call her. My mind was going in many directions wondering if the family was to blame for Marie's anxiety or if the mother's spirit was really the culprit.

My cell phone rang again and it was Deacon Tom. He told me he'd gotten a ride, would be arriving within five minutes, and I was to let the family know. His wife would be picking him up afterward because his car had to be towed. I again approached the family, told them the details of this delay, and got the same reaction as before. They wanted to speak to the other visitors and mourners themselves while, once again, having their talk with Mom.

As I passed the microphone, it gave off an annoying squeal of feedback. With the mike turned off, I had no idea how this could happen especially since it didn't occur when others walked by; just with me.

"Must be static in my hair or something," I thought. I checked the flower room doors once again and found them firmly secured.

As I walked through the chapel and into the lobby hall, I overheard a couple of people comment that they had heard an organ playing somewhere; the music on the CD didn't have any organ music in it. It was at this point that an ominous feeling began to rise in me because of the dead woman's strong nature in life. I felt she wasn't ready to give up the ghost yet.

I couldn't have been happier to see Deacon Tom get out of a cab that let him out at the back door of the mortuary. As I started to say hello to him, he dashed past me and into the office with his vestments, robe, and prayer book. He plopped those down, flew past me saying hi, paused to collect himself at the chapel's entry doors, and reverently walked in. He spoke with the family for a moment, and then addressed the group that had assembled for the rosary prayers. He sincerely apologized to all for his tardiness and let them know the rosary would start in five minutes.

As he dashed back my way, he grabbed my sleeve and asked for a quick cup of coffee. He drank it down and talked about how there was something funny about this whole affair.

As he put on his robe and vestments, he told me he'd been having nightmares ever since he agreed to recite the rosary prayers at this visitation. He'd had car trouble and *things* were happening in the church as well as at his home that made them all wonder who or *what* in the world they were dealing with.

"Oh, by the way, are *you* okay so far?" he asked in a fatherly manner. I said that I was and he patted me on the shoulder and gave me a kiss on my forehead, then he did the sign of the cross with his hand in front of my face while saying a blessing in Latin. This gave me the chills as Tom never recited in Latin. I knew for certain now that something wasn't right and jammed my hand into my pocket to feel my rosary.

Deacon Tom, in full vestments, walked down the aisle toward the casket. I knew he would turn the mike on himself, so I didn't worry about that. I did my job and turned off the CD player while also checking the settings in the sound booth at the back of the chapel for the microphone up front. All was as it should be, or so we thought.

As Tom approached the casket, a low electronic hum came out of the overhead speakers. I checked the frequency levels on the sound equipment but there was nothing I could change and nothing registered on the audio meters. I lowered the sound on the speakers to zero and they still hummed.

Tom began his blessing over the casket and the woman residing inside. It was a very moving and beautiful blessing, but was overshadowed by the annoyingly incessant hum. Several members of the group looked back at me working diligently to stop the irritating noise. All I could do was acknowledge their stares, shrug my shoulders, and keep trying. Deacon Tom approached the dais and the hum now turned into full feedback, blasting everyone's ears. He worked with the mike and the connections at the front of the chapel while I worked on the sound equipment in the back of the room. The feedback oddly and abruptly stopped. Tom and I could only look at each other with confused looks.

Tom began the rosary prayers. The equipment stayed quiet and seemed to work well until Tom got into the first decade of the rosary. The feedback returned even louder with the first Hail Mary. Again we worked together, all to no avail. He gave me the signal to totally cut the power to the mike, so I did. Tom used his booming voice, started the rosary again, and was able to complete it without aid of any electronic devices. We breathed a sigh of relief.

I noticed a car pull up and saw that Tom's wife was at the wheel. When I asked her to come in, she emphatically said, "No way!"

I returned and heard that the hum and a little bit of feedback had returned. I checked my equipment in the booth; the power was still off. I thought that something must be overloading the mike.

At the end of the rosary, Deacon Tom lovingly and thoughtfully said his good-byes to each member of the family and reverently walked out of the chapel. He then ran into the office, grabbed his stuff, and ran out of the funeral home, still wearing his robe and vestments.

"I pulled the damn cords out before I started the rosary!" he said as he entered the car, slamming the door on his robe. His wife put the car in drive and the two of them took off like bats out of hell, peeling out of the parking lot.

I went back into the building and turned the CD back on as per Marie's instructions. The music started, but it wasn't the right CD. I hadn't opened the player, yet this family's disc wasn't there. I wondered who was playing tricks as I looked everywhere and couldn't find the correct CD. I told the family their music was missing, but this didn't seem to faze them in the least. They let me know it was okay and that the music playing was a nice change from their mom's selected tunes.

About half past eight, people began to leave for the evening. I went into the office to look up what time her service was in the morning. There, in the file, in a *sealed* envelope, was the CD I had played earlier; the deceased had written "To Be Played at My Funeral" across the flap.

That was it for me. I wanted nothing more to do with this woman or her service. I counted my blessings that I wasn't assigned to the church service the next day. I closed the file and went out to ask the family to stay while I closed up. They were gone! An eerie feeling came over me and I checked the parking lot. Minutes earlier there were many cars in that parking lot—now, there was just mine. It was only twenty minutes to nine. I walked back into the building, to the lobby of the chapel, and knew I was alone with their deceased mother.

I took a deep breath and uttered a quiet prayer as I began my trek through the building to lock it down for the night. I started with the front door and the lights in the living room. I then walked determinedly through the back of the building, shutting down the workrooms and display areas, and ending in the kitchenette next to the office. Having turned off the coffee pot earlier, I was thankful that it was still off, but pulled the plug out of the wall just in case. At this point I noticed my hands shaking like dried leaves shivering on a dead tree limb.

After checking the bathrooms and hoping to barge in on a living human being, I carefully walked into the office to get my keys and purse. I did not want to have anything in my hands when I set the alarm, so I went out to my car and tossed everything onto the passenger seat. I closed and locked my passenger car door, took a moment to lean my head on the roof of my car, and became aware that my jaw was shaking, too. I had easily made the twenty-yard trek to my car, but dreaded turning around and going back into the building. I took a deep breath, turned around, and faced the open back door of the building.

My eyes were drawn to the left toward the flower room door that opens to the parking lot. I forced myself to look at the door; it was standing wide open. My feet felt like lead as I forced myself to approach it. Though located only a few yards to the left of the main door to the building, it felt as if it were miles away. As I approached the open door,

I saw it had been opened wide enough to jam it into the hedge behind it. I looked into the flower room; the room was dark. I grabbed the door and the knob and gave a hard tug that released it from the hedge. With trembling hands I turned the latch on the knob and shut the door. I gave it an extra tug just to be sure it was shut; it didn't budge.

I took another deep breath and walked back into the nearly dark mortuary. Almost in tears from fright and shaking like a leaf, the time I dreaded was upon me as I knew that the last room of lights I had to turn off was the chapel.

The light switches for the Blue Willows' chapel were located behind the casket and under a curtain. I did not want to turn off those lights, but that was my job and the security system wouldn't arm with the lights left on. I prayed as I entered the chapel, walked down the aisle, and approached the casket. After blowing out the candles at the head and the foot of the casket, I forced myself to look at the deceased. She lay there, quietly, as she should be. I walked under the curtains behind the casket to turn off the lights for the chapel and noticed light to my left coming from under the flower room's interior door.

Feelings of annoyance, anger, and utter foolishness began to overtake me in regard to these shenanigans. These emotions gave me the courage and strength to enter that room once again. As I opened the inner door to the flower room, I felt a cool breeze. Not only were the room's lights on, but the outer door was open again as well. It was only open about a foot or so, not jammed into the hedges like before, but this door thing got me ticked. I set my jaw, which no longer trembled, went into the room, shut and locked the outer door again, turned off the light, then shut and locked the inner door.

I went back to the wall panel to turn off the chapel lights and saw the candles lit again. Now, thoroughly angered and needing to stay that way, I blew out the candles once more, wet the smoldering wicks with my fingers, and took a minute to firmly look at the deceased woman.

With fists on my hips and a stern stare, forced calm and respect, I told her, "Stop it!" I went behind the casket, under the curtain, and turned off the lights. With my jaw firmly set, I quickly walked down the dark aisle toward the doors of the chapel, into the lobby, the alarm box, and freedom. I had just crossed the threshold of the chapel to the lobby, when the organ began to play.

My newfound courage left me. Uncontrollable tears and shivers of fright accompanied me as I turned off the last of the building's lights and set the alarm.

I got to my car with tears streaming down my face and found the courage for one last act of defiance. I yelled toward the building while unlocking my driver's side door, "Now, leave me the hell alone and don't follow me home. I've had it with you. You keep your butt here!" I got in my car to drive off and looked in my rearview mirror where I saw the silhouette of a woman in the back seat. I shook it off, blinked, looked back, and the image was gone.

When I got home, I told my husband and adult daughter about what had happened while trying to drink a cup of coffee. I had a hard time as I was shaking all over. Then things in my house began moving; stacks of books fell over, papers fell off tables. My cats ran out of the room and hissed at the ceiling. We saw a swirling flash of light go through the room, come around me, fade in and out, appear and disappear.

I got on the phone to a friend who is psychic and has dealt with this type of thing before. She said she had been waiting for me to call. She knew I was going to call and was in trouble. As I told her what was going on, she stopped me.

"The woman doesn't like you because you're not a good Catholic," she told me. "She was a very devout and controlling woman in life and still is in death. What did you bring home with you that's hers?"

When I said I had nothing, she yelled, "Look in your pockets. You brought something of hers home with you. She doesn't want you to have it." I looked in my jacket pockets, and lo and behold, found one of her memorial folders. I told my friend this, who then told me to get back in the car and return it to the funeral home, tonight!

I was tired and emotionally drained, but did as I was told. My daughter was kind enough to go with me. She acted gutsy and courageous on the drive back to the funeral home, suggesting that I just slide the folder under the door while trying not to trip the alarm, but I heard a slight catch in her voice that sounded like fear or nerves. I decided to take her advice, as well as tell the dead woman I was sorry for inadvertently taking with me what she felt to be her property. This scenario felt good; it felt right.

When we arrived at the funeral home, I stopped my car right in front of the door I had left through earlier and left the car running with the headlights on bright.

"Mom," my daughter said, "it's spooky here tonight. It's too quiet. Would you hurry up so we can get out of here? It doesn't feel right here." I did as she asked; moved my butt, slid the folder under the door as I crossed my fingers that the alarm didn't go off. That worked, so I said my piece, and went back to the car.

As I got in, my daughter asked, "Why is that door open?" She pointed her shaking finger toward the outer flower room door.

The door stood open almost all the way back to the bushes again. I shook with the mere thought of approaching the door another time. We sat paralyzed in the car and watched as it slowly moved and closed on its own. We didn't breathe or dare move as the opening grew narrower and narrower. With the car windows down, in the dead silence of the night, we heard the click of the latch when the door closed completely. The sounds of the night returned with the chirping of crickets and the call of a killdeer in the distance. We snapped out of our trance and peeled out of the parking lot just as the deacon's wife had done earlier.

Blue Willows is one funeral home that has had its share of frightening paranormal episodes. Angry or lost souls seem to be drawn there. Shortly after the incident with this overly controlling deceased woman, Marie quit. And as for Deacon Tom, when I spoke with him about the evening's antics, he laughed it off and said, "Sometimes, some folks just have to have the last word."

TIME TO CLOSE
THE CASKET

Dear friends, this now concludes our remembrances of those who have gone before us, but are still with us in many ways and many places.

To those who have passed who frighten us, chat with us, make us laugh, and make us cry, I salute and honor you. Thank you for honoring me with your presences, even when you made me angry or scared my socks off. Thank you for the flowers, thank you for the shivers, thank you for the laughter and the tears. Thank you for showing yourselves to me, whether in nightmarish dreams, sooty clouds, an unpaintable shadow on a wall, a full-on manifestation, or a disembodied voice. In many ways you have touched my heart and enriched my soul. Words of thanks are not enough to express my gratitude for all that you have given me, and now others as well.

On behalf of all who have chosen, for whatever reason, not to rest in peace, I'd like to thank you, one and all, for your literary attendance at these events. My heartfelt thanks go to each and every person who has read this book. Remember that as they were in life, so will they be in death. May they all rest in peace, when they're darn good and ready.

I bid you peace.

To Write to the Author

If you wish to contact the author or would like more information about this book, please write to the author in care of Llewellyn Worldwide Ltd. and we will forward your request. Both the author and publisher appreciate hearing from you and learning of your enjoyment of this book and how it has helped you. Llewellyn Worldwide Ltd. cannot guarantee that every letter written to the author can be answered, but all will be forwarded. Please write to:

Mariah de la Croix
℅ Llewellyn Worldwide
2143 Wooddale Drive
Woodbury, MN 55125-2989

Please enclose a self-addressed stamped envelope for reply,
or $1.00 to cover costs. If outside the U.S.A., enclose
an international postal reply coupon.

GET MORE AT LLEWELLYN.COM

Visit us online to browse hundreds of our books and decks, plus sign up to receive our e-newsletters and exclusive online offers.

- • Free tarot readings • Spell-a-Day • Moon phases
- • Recipes, spells, and tips • Blogs • Encyclopedia
- • Author interviews, articles, and upcoming events

GET SOCIAL WITH LLEWELLYN

 **Find us on Facebook**
www.Facebook.com/LlewellynBooks

Follow us on
 **twitter™**
www.Twitter.com/Llewellynbooks

GET BOOKS AT LLEWELLYN

LLEWELLYN ORDERING INFORMATION

Order online: Visit our website at www.llewellyn.com to select your books and place an order on our secure server.

Order by phone:
- • Call toll free within the U.S. at 1-877-NEW-WRLD (1-877-639-9753)
- • Call toll free within Canada at 1-866-NEW-WRLD (1-866-639-9753)
- • We accept VISA, MasterCard, and American Express

Order by mail:
Send the full price of your order (MN residents add 6.875% sales tax) in U.S. funds, plus postage and handling to: Llewellyn Worldwide, 2143 Wooddale Drive Woodbury, MN 55125-2989

POSTAGE AND HANDLING:

STANDARD: (U.S. & Canada)
(Please allow 12 business days)
$25.00 and under, add $4.00.
$25.01 and over, FREE SHIPPING.

INTERNATIONAL ORDERS (airmail only):
$16.00 for one book, plus $3.00 for each additional book.

Visit us online for more shipping options. Prices subject to change.

FREE CATALOG!

To order, call
1-877-
NEW-WRLD
ext. 8236
or visit our
website

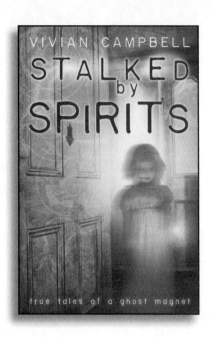

VIVIAN CAMPBELL

STALKED
by
SPIRITS

true tales of a ghost magnet

STALKED BY SPIRITS

True Tales of a Ghost Magnet

VIVIAN CAMPBELL

Haunted since childhood, Vivian Campbell has encountered angry wraiths, mischievous child spirits, terrorizing demons, and all sorts of bizarre, unearthly beings. Vivian relives these chilling and thrilling experiences in *Stalked by Spirits*, including how she and her family suffered violent phantom attacks, received small favors from a little girl ghost, negotiated with a demanding spirit, welcomed back a dearly departed pet, tolerated ghostly attendance at holiday dinners and Girl Scout meetings, and waged hair-raising battles with an evil entity threatening their baby daughter.

Taking us inside a variety of spirit-infested, often beautiful places—a stone mansion in the Tennessee mountains, a century-old college dorm, the first apartment she shared with her new husband, and the beloved Florida home that's been in her family for generations—these true tales vividly capture an extraordinary and haunted life.

978-0-7387-2731-8, 288 pp., 5³⁄₁₆ x 8   **$15.95**

MELBA GOODWYN

Chasing
Graveyard
Ghosts

INVESTIGATIONS
OF HAUNTED
AND
HALLOWED
GROUND

CHASING GRAVEYARD GHOSTS

Investigations of Haunted and Hallowed Ground

MELBA GOODWYN

Angry ghosts, malevolent red-eyed orbs, graveyard statues that come to life … Take a spine-tingling tour of haunted graveyards, from an incredibly active vampire burial site to Voodoo Queen Marie Laveau's wishing tomb.

Paranormal investigator Melba Goodwyn explores the ghostly phenomena, spooky legends, and frightful folklore associated with cemeteries. Fortified with her own hair-raising experiences, she offers insights into the graveyard ghosts and guardians, spirited statues, bizarre tombstone inscriptions, portals linking other dimensions, and ghost passageways along ley lines. There's also practical guidance for those who wish to investigate the many mysteries—paranormal and otherwise—that cemeteries hold.

978-0-7387-2126-2, 360 pp., 5 3/16 x 8   **$16.95**

To order, call 1-877-NEW-WRLD
Prices subject to change without notice
Order at Llewellyn.com 24 hours a day, 7 days a week!